THE RESTORATION OF LOVE

The Restoration of Love

W. ter Horst

Translated by
John Medendorp

WILLIAM B. EERDMANS PUBLISHING COMPANY
GRAND RAPIDS, MICHIGAN / CAMBRIDGE, U.K.

First published as *Eerherstel van de Liefde*,
by Uitgeversmaatschappij J. H. Kok b.v., Kampen, the Netherlands
© 1992 by J. H. Kok

English translation © 1997 Wm. B. Eerdmans Publishing Co.
255 Jefferson Ave. S.E., Grand Rapids, Michigan 49503 /
P.O. Box 163, Cambridge CB3 9PU U.K.

Printed in the United States of America

01 00 99 98 97   7 6 5 4 3 2 1

Library of Congress Cataloging-in-Publication Data

Horst, W. ter.
    The restoration of love / W. ter Horst.
        p.   cm.
    Includes bibliographical references (p.   ).
    ISBN 0-8028-4141-4 (pbk.: alk. paper)
    1. Love. 2. Love — Religious aspects — Christianity. I. Title.
BF575.L8H66   1997
177′.7 — dc21   96-47554
                                                    CIP

Contents

1. Introduction

Idle Musings?

For more than a year now I have walked around with the idea that I really should try to write a book about human love. A sort of *Ars amandi* (art of loving) for modern men and women who are seeking new paradigms, because the old ones have become unworkable. Yet nothing has ever come of it because it is too involved. What did I really have in mind? Were these not just idle musings? Then one day, during a televised report on an AIDS demonstration, the back of a man, about twenty-five years old, appeared on the screen. Close up. For three full seconds.

He was wearing a white jacket with the following message in black adhesive letters:

> Can we accept a society
> where we are deathly afraid
> to love?

What did he mean? I wanted to ask him, but he was anonymous. I could not even see his face, only the silver earring in his left ear. But his question stayed with me.

Was he suffering from the new plague? Was he HIV-positive? Was he defending love, a loved one, a friend? It had to be something like that. But what was he trying to say?

He apparently was among those who think all misery is a dysfunction of society. But what captured my interest is what he meant by *love*. Something important in his life, no doubt. He protested for it, and with

1

great care he had pasted those expensive adhesive letters on his jacket. He holds love in high regard and he does not want to be deathly afraid of it. And he is right. I am on his side.

But it occurred to me that the spread of the HIV virus has more to do with lovelessness than with love. That young man is sincere, and so am I. Yet we apparently mean two completely different things when we use the word love. That bothers me.

Idle musings or no, I must try. I can no longer refrain.

Would it be possible to bridge the gap between us?

"No, because it is a generation gap," Zeke asserted superficially, "and if you cannot accept that, call it a culture gap. Bridge it? Don't even try. Everyone has his own idea of love, and that is the way it should be. You should just stay out of it."

I simply cannot accept that, because I have it on good authority that love is for all people of all times and all places. Yet, there must then be, in spite of the generational and cultural differences, something essential, something abiding to say about love, in which we — common people — recognize ourselves, something that we can use.

Something!

"Love is like a kerosene lamp," Michael flippantly informed me. "Nostalgic and romantic, but inefficient, with the rank odor of soot. What you call love probably never existed. And even if it did, it does not exist anymore. Be real. There is only sex, self-interest, and the fear of being alone and actually seeing yourself for what you are. So people are sometimes forced to come to some kind of understanding. There is nothing wrong with that, but do not use that deceptive word 'love'. Call it friendship if you want."

"Power," Sandra replied angrily. "What they call love is really just a power play that men use to keep their women under their thumbs, to keep them from finding their true selves. You are an experienced psychotherapist, you know that as soon as the woman no longer accepts her submissive role, love just does not cut it anymore."

I sputtered something back, but she was not to be denied. I could not blame her. She had experienced horrible things. But why did she not at least test her experiences against those of others?

She had, she said, and that was precisely why she no longer wanted anything to do with it. Women's solidarity — now that was something she could believe in. And yet . . .

Walter looked at me and gave me a cynical laugh. "You are making it too difficult," he said. "You and your love. You have to know life a little. Why would you buy a cow when you can get milk everywhere? Free, too, if you know how to maneuver a little and don't have too many scruples."

I continued to probe, because he was not the first to express this opinion. I told him that I planned to write a book about love. He looked at me with surprise and could not for the life of him figure out what I could possibly want to say about love. At the very most something like, "One hundred opening lines and sixty tricks of the trade for beginning and experienced lovers, with detailed instructions and application tips."

Then he added for extra measure, "Don't even start. *Talking about love provokes hate.*"

That was certainly not what I wanted.

And then there was Frank. He holds human love in very high regard, or so he claimed. Love is nice, but . . .

But "There are more important things. Public affairs, divine affairs. They supersede self-interest. Human love has to be sacrificed on the altar of the sublime."

What now? Zeke is superficial, Michael is flippant, Sandra is angry, Walter is cynical, and Frank plays the part of the keeper of the sublime.

In this way I attempt to brush them off. The gap that separates me from them also appears to be unbridgeable. Too far to shout, let alone converse. The distance is too great. We are speaking different languages. Even when we use the same words, they have different meanings. Forget about them. What does it matter, anyway?

And yet I cannot brush them off so easily. *They too are creatures of flesh and blood, each with a story to tell. I am one of them.* If dialogue between us on the subject of love is no longer even possible, we are in grave danger.

They are not, after all, crazy or stupid. They are not just talking nonsense. They do not think of themselves as superficial, flippant, angry, cynical, or sublime. That is just my opinion of them, for my own peace of mind. That is why they must be taken just as seriously as the young man in the white jacket with the adhesive letters. Later, I will meet them all again, even the young man in the white jacket.

Restoration

The above presents, above all, a statement of the problem of this book.

It is my conviction that we must bring this denigration of love to a halt. More strongly put, *love must be restored to its place of honor*. It must receive its due again, be esteemed again.

To this I want to make my own contribution — aware of my limited frame of reference, but willing to stick out my neck a little, to attempt, whether I succeed or not, to say something essential, something enduring about love, something in which common people can recognize themselves, something they *can use* in times like these. Something.

If I apply myself to the task, which now seems likely, then it will become clear to me what that something is. I must try, in any case, because I believe in love. Holy love.

"Don't even get started," Sandra said. "Men do not know what love is."

That may be, but I nevertheless believe that I have experienced something of love. Besides, one can always consult others.

"And what do you mean by 'common people'?"

"Simply those who speak the language."

Can It Be Put into Words?

On another level, I have asked myself whether a book like this is really the best medium for imparting anything essential about love. Would a story not be better, or a poem, or music, a play, a sculpture or a painting?

In our times we have witnessed a tremendous inflation of words. In the last century, "great words" have been used too often and too easily, words that appear to be worth nothing when it comes right down to it and leave people disillusioned.

And that is not all. There are realities that do not allow themselves to be captured in the fishnet of language. We generally lack well-defined words for these realities, words that express precisely what we mean. And so we must rely on words that point to meanings and experiences; poetic, mythic, symbolic words. These have a (sub)cultural and sometimes even a personal character, and they are not always easily understood. Writing about love is a risky endeavor.

4

Osmosis

I periodically gaze with admiration at the painting of Gustav Klimt — especially *The Kiss* (see the front cover), which is found in the Austrian Gallery of Art in Vienna. It measures 1.8 by 1.8 meters, gold on linen, and was painted in 1907-8.

Klimt is one of the Viennese artists from the short-lived movement known as Art Nouveau.[1] A great deal can be said about this movement, both positive and negative, but that is not related to our subject.

What fascinates me here is that Klimt — in his own extravagant way, with the motifs and themes of his circle and with his own personal fascination with gold — tries to reveal something of what love is. Something, not everything. Something that transcends all incidental and personal experiences.

He grasps, as it were, the osmotic moment. The peak experience of absolute devotion to one another in trust, and thereby the knowledge of the other in the deepest recesses of being. Not dissolving the self, nor surrendering the self, but coming to oneself through and to each other.[2]

The lovers possess for each other a certain supernatural beauty. They suddenly find themselves in a blooming spring meadow. Everything around them is transparent gold. Angels playing soft music on harps and violins and the scent of almond blossoms may be part of the fantasy as well (although Richard

---

1. The Viennese practitioners of Art Nouveau around the time of the "Sezession" were occupied in their day (1910) with the thought of Schopenhauer, who attributed to art, especially music (Wagner), a transcendental function. They believed that art had the ability to reveal something allegorically above and beyond the methods of metaphysics. The influence of Ludwig Wittgenstein must also be mentioned. He published his well-known work *Tractatus Logico-Philosophicus* in 1918, the year of Klimt's death (and not in 1929 as is often assumed). I am not entirely comfortable with Schopenhauer and Wagner — nor Nietzsche for that matter — but I must admit that they were on an interesting, albeit dangerous, trail.

2. *Osmosis,* a term that refers in the natural sciences to membrane diffusion, is used in this book in the sense of a mutual interpenetration of experiences. At certain points I almost arrive again at the original scientific meaning, when referring to the mixing of bodily fluids through the membrane of the skin. The skin can be viewed, as far as I am concerned, as a boundary for love. I view every attempt to break through it as a violent attack on personal integrity.

Clayderman and the scent of Chanel No. 5 will suffice if preferred). "But things are not quite so profound the next day," Kloos poeticized.[3] Love contains more than osmotic moments. We will not ignore that fact in this book. In addition to the peak experiences, there are also lowland, valley, and even abyss experiences in love.

There are people who never get over such experiences. For them *The Kiss* of Gustav Klimt is nothing but an overly romantic, noisy painting of two hysterical people sitting in a sleeping bag at the edge of the abyss attempting something needlessly difficult.

In the seventies, Klimt was very popular among students. Then he was vilified for a few years, and now there is a certain inclination toward him again. I like him. He is attempting to reveal something.

Fishnet

It seems to me that the intent of this book is now evident and that the tone has been set. What must still be done in an introductory chapter is to sketch out the author's frame of reference. By this I mean — to use an old example — the net with which he fishes the waters of reality. What is caught depends on the shape of the net, the size of the mesh, the methods of the fisherman, and the place where he casts his net. When the frame of reference is made known, it becomes clear which choices have been made. That may save some time and effort. For if the aspiring reader has no interest in the book, he can readily put it back on the shelf.

My frame of reference is strongly influenced by my profession, orthopedagogy, the science that studies problems of upbringing. Problems of upbringing have different causes and therefore require different remedies. That notion is present throughout this book.

Furthermore, I have always been very fascinated by the difficulties and possibilities of *everyday life*. After all, that is where the problems are experienced, and that is where we must first seek a solution.[4]

3. Willem Kloos, ed., *Heinrich Heine* (Amsterdam, 1906).
4. See my *Algemene orthopedagogiek* [General orthopedagogy], 2nd ed. (Kampen, 1981),

The most important core words which form my frame of reference are *heart, person, experience, dialogue, freedom,* and *creature.* The last word here implies a relatedness to and responsibility toward things, plants, animals, and of course, people. It also means responsibility toward the Creator. So stated, we have said too much and too little. We will not entirely lose sight of the wide, cosmic expanse of love, yet we will primarily be concerned with *human* love in this book.

Within one's frame of reference there are also *personal experiences* which continually interact with it. As a result, some will understand most aspects of a subject like this very well, while at the same time understanding others very little, or not at all. That is inevitable, but it compels us to circumspection and thus leaves little room for dogmatism.

I became very aware of that while reading a book by Anja Meulenbelt: *Casablanca, of de onmogelijkheden van de heteroseksuele liefde* (Casablanca, or the impossibilities of heterosexual love). Of course, one who walks around with the idea of writing a book about the restoration of love immediately comes into conflict with such a book. I thought reading her book might perhaps spare me the effort of writing my own.

Sometimes I liked what I read, and sometimes I did not. For example, she writes, "Not only do I believe in the ideal of love between equals, I will not make do with less. I do not have to make do with less. There is nothing wrong with the ideal. There is something wrong with the reality." I agree whole-heartedly. And a little later, she continues, "I know, nevertheless, that it is possible, an equal relationship with a man, love in which you can give yourselves over to each other without the one having to give up her individuality for it, a relationship without power struggles — not over the dishes, not over the kids, not over money, not over how much attention the other one gets, not over the room the other needs in order to remain himself."[5]

That moved me and encouraged me. We have more or less the same ideal and the same experience. But my story and therefore the frame of reference from which I intend to illuminate the phenomenon of love is

---

which contains mostly theoretical considerations. See also my *Het herstel van het gewone leven* [The restoration of the common life], 4th ed. (Groningen, 1988), which is directed especially to the practice of everyday life.

5. Anja Meulenbelt, *Casablanca* (Amsterdam, 1990), pp. 12-14.

completely different. And so she sees things that must remain hidden to me.[6]

I will describe my own experiences briefly and in much less detail. My account is admittedly reserved, but in a book like this, honesty demands that it not be withheld.

I have never lacked where love is concerned. There were a few unsuccessful attempts at what I like to call "forming a love covenant." That caused a good deal of heartache, but it was never due to loveless-ness; at most powerlessness, perhaps misunderstanding. I had normal, loving parents. Grew up during the war. Left home at seventeen, because I had to earn money and wanted to be independent. Married at thirty-one with Annie. Have had unbearable grief, concern, sickness and death, but never a lack of love. When she died, I decided after the initial chaos to remain alone, so that I would not have to lose anyone again. But Els brought light back into my life. And how!

Around me, among my nearest kin, I have never actually experienced anything grim where love is concerned. My nine uncles were without exception quiet, everyday, dependable men, who worked hard. It was for them a point of honor that their wives no longer had to work them-selves to the bone at the textile factory or as maids. Moreover, they were keen that their children have more education than they had. In order to provide that, they set aside their pipe tobacco and their Saturday glass of beer for as long as was necessary.

My father was also one who, like all the men of his family, got up early, cleaned out and relit the stove, filled the coal bin, and shined the shoes. The men and the older boys naturally did these things. (Who else is supposed to do it? Your mother?)

My aunts were loving, caring, but very resolute figures, who kept things in good order and met their husbands "halfway," as we say in the family.

That is all. Nothing special. Everything very boring/comfortable/predictable. Cross out what does not suit your fancy. Normal, intertwined couples, about whom nothing else will ever be written.

I know professionally, and by word of mouth, horrible accounts of repressive men and their submissive wives who sacrifice themselves and

6. Meulenbelt has evocatively described her experiences in detail in *De schaamte voorbij* [Beyond shame], published in 1977.

8

never come into their own right. I did not, however, grow up with them; I have never experienced them personally. It even surprises me when I am told about such people.

I have also heard tales of women who publicly shame their husbands because they are not pleased with their sexual performance or with the amount of money they are earning. We do not speak very readily of such problems these days. And yet they exist and there are those who suffer from them. Any social worker knows of such cases. But again, for me it is knowledge about, not knowledge of, and certainly no experience of such things.

In a book like this, honesty demands that I go deeper, so as not to lead the reader astray. Behind a person's experiences lies another region. What might that be? The essential person? The ground of being? The heart, I prefer to say. There where the Great Longing dwells. That which remains of one's *sense of direction* — high in the light of the snowcaps or in the deep darkness of the abyss — when one moves beyond explanation.

For me that is — I write it with fear and trembling because it sounds so pretentious, evokes the wrong associations, and because it actually is ineffable — for me that is the dream, the vision of the Messianic Kingdom, the Kingdom of Love, where *all people and all things are handled with respect for their own nature,* and thus come into their own right.

Readers who find this all to be rather heavy are asked, before they set aside this book, at least to read Chapter 5, which is entitled "Clear-Obscure."

Moralism

This intent and this frame of reference both suffer inevitably from a certain *moralism.*

For me, morals do not consist of a group of rules that are prescribed by tradition or some higher power. They are rather a group of practical means that produce a *desired end.* The desirability of the end will be placed under scrutiny in this book, and the means will be humbly recommended.

Those who object can now no longer say that they were not warned.

2. A Perilous Interjection

Wait a Minute

"Look before you leap, then you won't have to repent later," my wise old grandmother always used to say. And she ought to know. The Land of Love that we seek to enter is full of mysterious dangers and unexpected risks. Those who do not know the lay of the land should not rush in. As they say: "Act in haste, repent in leisure."

At the grey stone portal that gives entry to the Land of Love hang heavy oak doors adorned with small, softly glowing gold and silver figures. Before the doors stands the doorkeeper with hand aloft. He controls the mysterious power of metamorphosis.

At times he is the concerned parent: "No, my daughter, not you. Those who enter here do not return" (sometimes, in retrospect, that is not so bad).

Then again he is an old, wise Stoic, shaking his head: "Be attached to nothing and no one."

He can also take the form of the sublime priest, or the priestess of some unearthly religion: "Raise your eyes to heaven and set your heart on high, for it is not to be found here below."

For those who are less discreet, he is a drunken sailor: "Trust no one, trust no one, love is nothing but a mirage, you're better off gettin' knockdown drunk."

Many other forms are possible — most recently even that of the sociologist, for the doorkeeper is a resourceful and trendy wizard. Yet his message is always that of Grandma. Sometimes even stronger. There is no denying such wisdom. And so we will not ignore the warnings, but will consider them doubly important. Nevertheless, we will still enter that mysterious portal, full of expectation, for traces of irresistible sounds and scents are continually coming our way. They come from the Land of Enchantments, where a man loves instinctively, from the loins; and from the Garden of Desires, that of Hieronymous Bosch — and from the Garden of Love, the one portrayed by Rubens.

Frequently we hear the songs of the troubadours, but their courtly love is not meant for us.

Yet the old Court of Desire must still be out there somewhere, the one sung of in the thirteenth-century poem *The Romance of the Rose (Le roman de la rose)*. Lord Pleasure dances there and Lady Jubilee sings all day. It is also said that the fountain of Narcissus is to be found there and that Eros feels very much at home.

In the distance we also hear the cult hero, pop star Lenny Kravitz, sing about his own garden: "In this garden, this lovely garden, I build a temple of love." Very alluring.

And then we detect scents and sounds from the distant, hidden *Garden of Gardens*. Delightful scents of balsam, nard, and cinnamon. Shulamite herself, the royal shepherdess, is the High Priestess of Love. She dances and sings the Song of Songs. With her, lovers come into their own right, in that they are able to gaze upon one another's true nature, illumined by the Star of Hope and warmed by the Fire of the Lord.

It is that garden, the one that the ancient tales say lies hidden in the Land of Love, that we want to reach.

Yet we are hardly through the door when we notice something. Grandma and the doorkeeper were right. The Land of Love is full of dangers. Halewijn, friend of the elves, rides round, full of deadly desire.[1] He sings beautiful, irresistible songs and takes delight in snatching away the lives of the young girls who come to him. Now and again there is a king's daughter, who makes him a head shorter. But in no time at all, he is riding around the hills again on his white horse with an aggrieved look on his face. He sings a little ditty, and all who hear him want to be with him, in spite of it all.

On the road that leads to the Land of Enchantments and the gardens stands the House of Testing. It is inhabited by a beautiful, sadistic

---

1. Halewijn is a wizard of lore who by his song lured noble women to their death. He was himself finally outsmarted and decapitated by the daughter of a king.

princess — a man eater! First she bewitches men. Then she gives them unsolvable riddles and impossible tasks. He who does not succeed is mercilessly emasculated and can be thankful that he is set free and not kept to do dishes forever in a somber, drafty kitchen.

From time to time there appears the tailor's apprentice, who in his simple innocence proves to be too clever. Whether the lad finds happiness is not known. But no matter; the princess always outlives him and begins her sweet little life all over again.

In the Land of Love, good-looking princes become foul, smelly beggars, and wart-filled toads become handsome princes — if only they receive a kiss with their breakfast.

Some Papageno nearly dies of heart failure from the foul potion that is given him, but then walks around hand in hand, ecstatic with the same adorable Papagena, whistling with the birds.[2] In itself that appears rather convenient, but the danger is that these creative transformations all too often never take place. That has brought many to misery.

The house of Bluebeard stands off at a distance. Everything is in perfect order — beautiful garden, nice car. Fine man, that Bluebeard.[3] Ideal son-in-law. Nothing unusual about him. Those modern women don't know how good they have it.

Danger threatens everywhere. What are we doing here? The Garden of Gardens appears unreachable. Exasperated, we seek shelter at the Forest Inn.

At the bar sit Don Juan and Giacomo Casanova (or Sir John and Jake Newhouse) facing each other and exchanging stories of the number of wild women they have managed to bring under their spell. "Scoring" they call that nowadays. The more they can sexually humiliate a woman, the more they like it. Just give her a boot in the rear, and she will always think nostalgically of that sweet, unhappy boy, and will believe that she is the only one with whom he ever knew a moment of intimacy. The great lovers look at each other triumphantly.

We flee to the sitting room. But there sings none other than Marlene

2. Papageno, a character from Mozart's opera *The Magic Flute*, desires Papagena, but fails the initiation trials that will join him with her in a perfect union. Although the couple fails to attain perfect love like their counterparts, Tamino and Pamina, they remain together, representing ordinary human love.

3. Bluebeard, also a figure of lore, was known for marrying and killing one wife after another.

Dietrich, with her smokey voice: "I am made of love from head to toe. That is my world, and nothing more." In the meantime she helps an eccentric professor get skunked. That is of course more than I can bear. Outside again! "But in The Forest are the hunters, who hunt rapaciously, yes, yes."

Actually, we all know it from the time we are knee-high to a grasshopper. In this land, if one is to reach the Garden of Gardens, one needs something to make one immune to spells and charms. But what? A good road map? A pair of glasses to see things differently? (Later it will become clear that we have simply taken the wrong road and have ended up in a rather obscure area of the Land of Love.)

3. Secrets of the Heart

Deep

Ancient wisdom tells us that true love has to do with the heart. It has been heartily sung on many an occasion. The world's languages contain innumerable expressions and sayings to that effect — from "heartfelt" to "heartrending." Bakeries sell heart-shaped cakes on Mother's Day. We find this primitive intuition engraved in the bark of some stately beech tree: "You are the love of my heart. I know it *deep* down inside, at the core of my being, in my innermost part, there, *in my heart*, that is where I know it, want it and feel it; more intensely than I could ever put into words. I love you."

Is that all simply a manner of speaking, with no real reference? An overly romantic way of describing things? A worn out and therefore useless image? Is it just adolescent flattery, or another vile means of getting women under one's spell and conquering them? Or are we perhaps dealing here with a deeper, rock-hard truth of human existence?

If the latter is the case — as I am convinced it is — then the heart must be restored not only to our thought and speech about love, but also to the consummation of our love, to the *process* of love. For what use is a loving heart if my lover and others, if animals, the plants and my surroundings, never notice anything different about me except that I speak eloquently and sing movingly about love?

Fringe Word

Suddenly we are overwhelmed with questions.

Regarding the heart itself: what kind of entity is it, really?

Regarding the relation of the heart to the other forms of existence: the heart is called the innermost part; but then how is it related to the outermost part?

Is the heart love itself? If not, how are they related? How can it be reached, and how can heartbreak be avoided?

Reflection only serves to multiply our questions, and we must take care not to pursue the many highly interesting but tangential issues that do not contribute to the purpose of this book.

Heart is a word that stands at the fringe of our existence and extends over the whole of our human powers of imagination and comprehension. The word simultaneously reveals and hides a mystery; and for that reason is rightly a symbol. In the first chapter we referred to it as life's deepest level, the core of the human person. "There where the Great Longing dwells. That which remains — high in the light of the snowcaps, or in the deep darkness of the abyss — when one moves beyond explanation."[1] To this we can add that the heart holds together the various parts of our lives, makes them a whole, integrates them. It is to our heart that we point to when we want to refer to ourselves — not to our head.

I am not able to put it into sharper relief. Others may be able to state it in a more eloquent way, but not in a more exact way.

The understanding that *there is a heart, and yet that it is something other than what we comprehend it to be* is as old as self-consciousness.

I imagine that when they had to find a word for the blood pump, that hollow muscle that provides the body with blood, they also very appropriately named it *heart,* due to its well-perceived similarity to the real heart. Am I inverting the sequence? It really does not matter, so long as we, in heaven's name, remember that we are dealing with a fringe word. If we fail to remember that fact, the real heart becomes a metaphor, some sort of figure of speech, a figment of our imagination. Something for poets, philosophers, and chit-chats. Not something to honor, respect, or listen to.

---

1. This is a wordplay on the title of an article that appeared in H. Coenen, et al., *Door kou bevangen; Zelfdoding en nabestaanden* [Overcome by the cold: Suicide and the survivors] (Baarn, 1990).

15

There, in the heart, are hidden the deepest human motives. I prefer to call it The Great Longing. An inborn, vague, nearly undefinable desire. Yet, for what?

To be truly *human:* that is our destination, nothing else. All people desire to come *into their own right.* They want their *true nature* to come to light. They long for love, happiness, peace, wholeness, righteousness. These are words that speak to me in this connection, and on which I am willing to gamble, because I have experienced something of them in my heart of hearts.

In my heart of hearts: because nothing is in the heart that is not first in the senses and the ego. Except the Great Longing, of course. Yet it remains dormant so long as it is not disturbed. This needs to be said, but it cannot be elaborated at this point (see Chapter 8, "Shulamite"). The senses and the ego receive enough attention these days. They must wait now. First the heart.

In the heart, at the crossroads of life, the decisive, great yearnings are found. It is important for us to pursue this further, since we will assert below that true love is one of these yearnings.

Supra

There is a manner of speaking that tends to place the head and the heart in opposition to one another. That seems to me not only careless, but inaccurate, and therefore dangerous. The head stands for the rational and intellectual in such cases, and the heart for the intuitive and emotional.

Taking it yet a step further, the heart comes to designate the irrational. If that were indeed the case, I would have to advise you all not to engage the heart at the crossroads of life, since the irrational is the place of bewitching and spells: that of Halewijn, Bluebeard, and their kin.

The heart is just the opposite of the irrational. "The heart has its own reasons which Reason does not know," Pascal strikingly says.[2] If the heart is engaged, the self-consciousness (and therefore reality-consciousness)

---

2. *Pascal's Pensées,* with an English translation, brief notes and introduction by H. F. Stewart (New York: Modern Library, 1947), pp. 342-43.

works at full throttle. All systems go! Full of possibilities. Complete integration.

What goes on in the heart, therefore, is not irrational, but *supra-rational*, above reason.

It is a *knowing* that, after having thought all things through carefully, leaves behind reasoning and arguments.

It is also a *willing* and a *choosing* which, after consideration of all the pros and cons, and after a similar searching of the conscience, rises above all of these, suddenly or gradually, in a crossroads *decision.*

The same is true of *feeling.* Here too all things are thoroughly felt, nothing suppressed or denied. Then comes openness and clarity.

The heart works *supra,* or over, the entire extent of being. When the heart is engaged, the person comes as close to the total self as is possible. Such an engagement of the heart always remains with a person, even after many years when nothing more of it can be remembered.

In retrospect, when we are back on our feet and back at half speed, we can hardly imagine that we ourselves were responsible for such an experience. And in fact, I do not believe we are.

Oversimplification?

We have now reached a dangerous point in our attempt at the Restoration of Love. Suddenly everything seems so simple. It is, after all, ancient wisdom, older than civilization itself: the heart! (Why didn't we think of that before?) Engage the heart, apply it! The rest takes care of itself. Love is restored to its place of honor; it has regained its value and worth by returning the heart to its rightful place. *Fini!*

If we were to think thus, we would be as limited in our thinking as the young man in the white jacket. He sees all misery as a dysfunction of society. His error is that he is simply parroting others, who first shrink reality until they find some truth that they can handle, and then loudly aver that reality is really just that simple. (They confuse the result of methodological reduction with the full truth regarding existence, which is always other than what we are able to comprehend. That is not to say that they have not managed in the course of things to latch onto some isolated piece of reality. Problems with love, for example, can indeed also be attributable to a society that "alienates"

17

its members; from themselves, from each other; from plants, animals and things; and from God.)

We will try in so far as it is possible to avoid oversimplification.

Filters

First we must engage and apply ourselves to the terms once again.

Whatever else may come to light regarding love, it is of greatest importance that the heart "be engaged and applied." I will not under any circumstances dilute the expression. But in order to engage the heart, both our own and that of others, it must first be accessible.

Accessibility is an enormous problem, older than civilization itself. We already hear in primeval tales of cold, hard, restless and deceitful hearts. Supposedly, there are even heartless people, although that seems to contradict what we claimed above.

We cannot just open our hearts to anyone or anything. It is the most vulnerable part of our being. We must not allow too much harm to come to our heart, since it would be unbearable. For that reason, in the course of our childhood development, a couple of protective regions form around the heart: that of the "senses" and the "ego." They function as *filters*, so to speak, which protect the heart from too much pain.

But sometimes things go amiss. The filters are not yet sufficiently strong or selective, the heart is extra sensitive, or the attack to which it is subject is exceptionally fierce. Then the pain is greater than the heart can bear. This type of experience also stays with a person, even when he can later remember nothing of it. If a person happens to lack vitality at such a moment, the heart surrenders its integrating function and the person "falls to pieces." That is called "disintegration." The dialogue with reality in which the person participates is broken off. The person falls into the inaccessible world of confusion. Thus nothing from outside can encroach on the inside. (Nor can anything inside reach the outside.)

Everyone has such a breaking point. Life can be so rough that we become nearly or completely crazy.

If the personality possesses vitality, the heart partially or completely encapsulates itself in order to protect itself from a fatal recurrence. In this way the heart can continue to exercise its integrating function.

Nevertheless, an impenetrable area, a sort of defensive plug, appears in the filter: "Don't even talk to me about that. That is an old wound. I am extra sensitive on that point. *I cannot self-assuredly respond to that; I can only compulsively react.*" Examples of such plugs are fear of abandonment, mistrust, problems with authority, prejudices, and so on. These are called *dressaten* by the Individual Psychologists.[3] Fixed, stereotypical, defensive reactions, learned through pain and shame, which limit the freedom of action. The word "neuroses" is far too heavy for this.

"How Does It Taste?"

Nicole goes completely berserk whenever her cooking does not measure up in some way. "How does it taste?" she would ask menacingly. Martin and the kids are well aware of this, and stumble all over each other to declare that it is once again absolutely delicious. But she knows very well that they are lying. Then she makes a scene and the rest of the day, and a couple of nights as well, are very uncomfortable. "I know very well that you think I am a bad housewife and a bad mother. One of these days I'm going to leave; then you'll be happy. You hate me!"

During a break in the storm they can even sometimes laugh about it, but every time something goes wrong, or if she thinks it has gone wrong, she reacts in the same, stereotypical, *irrational* manner.

To whom was she really reacting? Not to Martin and the children.

Even she is not sure. It probably has something to do with her late father, she thinks, whom she remembers as a real bully, who would mercilessly berate her mother over the slightest little detail in the housekeeping in her presence. Her mother, however, has a very different image: "Your father was very easy to get along with," she insists.

---

3. Individual Psychology is the method employed by persons such as Alfred Adler and F. Kuenkel, who were active at the turn of the century. They were students of Freud, but departed from Freud in ways that were pedagogically more useful. The method has, lamentably, fallen out of fashion.

Everyone has such defenses, which obstruct access to the heart. The younger the person is when they appear, the deeper they are lodged and the more difficult they are to remove, since they have become, so to speak, a part of the personality. That can be rather burdensome, for ourselves and for our loved ones, even though our loved ones often become sensitive to the problem.

Armor

There are also, however, those unhappy folk who have had to enclose their hearts *completely* in the armor of bitterness at a very young age in order to protect themselves from disintegration. Their senses and ego are closed; their heart cannot be reached. It appears to be made of stone. That which once saved them from disintegration now hinders them. They are like medieval knights who are unable to lay down their armor after the battle.

Something very special has to take place in order to coax them out of their armor, naked and vulnerable, to begin a new life. All the time that their heart was enclosed in armor, their senses and ego did not develop. They were, after all, unneeded. The armor functioned as a sort of facade of maturity. Now they have nothing. Without the cumbersome armor they are as vulnerable as a newborn baby.

"Come out of your armor, my love."

"I don't dare!"

"Why not?"

"Because of the big, bad wolf!"

And though we say that the big, bad wolf has been caught by the woodsman and will see neither moon nor sun . . . we know that it is not true.

Often they are difficult people; incapable of giving and receiving love. Sometimes they are awful people, because they are always seeking justification for their armor and therefore find all kinds of ways to ensure that they are hated and let down. Or even worse, they look for reasons to say, "See? Love is just an illusion!"

I occasionally comfort myself with the thought that their hearts are not really made of stone, but are — under that rock-hard, cruel, impenetrable armor of aversion, bitterness, vengefulness and hate — as tender and innocent as a baby's heart. A very sentimental thought, no doubt. But how else should I deal with my sense of inadequacy in dealing with such people?

Neglect

This armor of the heart is ascribed to early childhood neglect.

In order to avoid this, it is not so important that the child be scrubbed and tucked into a clean bed. In itself, that does not mean very much, even though I have always maintained that good pedagogics begins with clean underwear. But smelly places can very well be warm places, and where hygiene is strictly maintained can often be a very cold place.

Early childhood neglect takes place *when there is something amiss with love.* That is the point here. Spoiling, therefore, is also a form of neglect. Only in an atmosphere of loving protection and respect for growing independence can a child develop the filters of personality. If that does not occur, the defenses regularly appear or the armor develops.

The parents, or the single mother or father, must have something left over for the child. (We will later call this *élan vital*). Sometimes there is just not enough. Perhaps because the parents are too young and still have to invest too much in themselves. It can also be that there is something else in their lives that makes love impossible. All of us — married or unmarried — must ask ourselves if we really want a child, or whether we really want something else.

Sometimes people have children in order to fill a void in their lives — to atone for a marriage gone bad, or to provide a "bundle of joy" for a lonely, miserable woman.

Not a Dog . . . a Child!

The director of the Home for Underage, Unwed Mothers and Children called me up several years ago late one evening, and asked whether I could come immediately. A drunken man had come and wanted to take a child along with him.

He was not really drunk, but he really wanted a child.

"You have so many of them here that those little tarts don't even know what to do with them all," he stubbornly repeated over and over again, "and I just thought . . ."

"Take your coat off and then let's sit down so you can tell me all about it," I said.

A moving love story. Married about fifteen years. After a couple of miscarriages, having lost all courage, they both buried themselves in the business. "Her business! Women's clothing! She is very good at it. We do everything together, even at home, and we were — no, damn it, we are! — a good couple."

Five years ago his wife suddenly slipped away into some sort of depression, with delusions and suicidal tendencies. She was hospitalized, and they submitted to intensive marriage therapy. In those days the spouse was automatically made to feel at fault. The opposite should have occurred, since he was already bursting with guilt feelings. Soon enough, out of misery and loneliness, he went out on his wife a couple of times, for which he would never forgive himself. Three long years they lived with worry, in hope and fear. They drastically cut back the business and began a new life. Then came two reasonably good years. "We had come through the worst and we still had each other, and that was the most important thing. What would we do without each other?"

Two weeks prior, however, she had begun to slip away again, slowly but unmistakably. On his way home, he felt a sense of dread in his heart. He did not know what he would find, and he was afraid that he would not be able to avoid hospitalizing her again.

He did not have the courage to go home. "I just have to do something," he thought. After a drink here and a drink there, he came up with the idea of buying a dog. That would cheer her up.

But hey, what's a dog? Then a line from a long-forgotten song stuck in his mind: "What joy! A child to us is born!" That was the solution! He could have kicked himself. Of course. A child!

That was why he was here. And he'd be damned if he was going to leave without a child to save his love and himself from destruction.

22

Such unhappy people are out to find more love, but that only happens with children when the parents are first able to provide, on a continual basis, an abundance of the same.

There are also women who say, "Partners come and go, but a child stays. That is why I want a child but not a man. The truly permanent, deeply satisfying relationship is between the mother and the child." That is a dry rationale of which I, as an orthopedagogue, am deeply afraid. If a child must take the place of a partner, symbiosis and incest are lying in wait.

Sun and Moon

Where love is concerned, children are just like moons that reflect the light of the sun. If the sun does not shine on them, they remain in the dark. If the sun shines too brightly, they are scorched. When the sun shines normally, the little moon shines along with it, and then the child can become, somewhere between the years of seven and eleven, a little sun at home.

But that is temporary. During the following period of growing independence, the average child becomes a capricious planet, having apparently lost all of its own fire. During this period, the parents can be glad when the child wants to reflect a little of the parental sunshine. For the first time, the parents love their growing children more than the other way around. That is good too, because otherwise life would be unbearable. But many parents suffer from the fact that their grown-up children provide them so little sun, and yet are so little moon. That does not matter; if children receive their share of sunshine before their seventh year, the investment will undoubtedly produce a return, even though the dividend is not always paid to the parents.

Only adults can be sun and moon for each other. And who is an adult before their thirtieth birthday nowadays?

(Astronomically, of course, none of this makes any sense, but mythologically the image is correct. The mysterious, softly glowing silver and gold figures on the oak doors of the entrance to the Land of Love are — if we take a closer look — the sun and the moon. Gold suns and silver moons.)

If a small, vulnerable child receives love from her parents in an ambiguous way, the child must, perforce, protect her heart with armor. Some parents are not very easy to figure out. They can be capricious and undependable: almost suffocating when the moment is right, and distant when the child needs them — and for that reason untrustworthy, with a cold voice and one eye glued to the television: "Yes, Johnny, stop whining, you know we love you." Or prostituting themselves: "I love only you, as long as you pay me handsomely for it" (with good behavior).

Relative Neglect

This may not be an orthopedagogical conclusion, but we must now draw attention to *relative neglect*.

There are children who receive an optimal upbringing. They are neither neglected nor spoiled. They are loved and strong, protected and challenged. And yet their hearts are accessible only with difficulty or not at all. From the very beginning things do not go very well. The reason for it is not entirely clear. Some experts appeal to slight brain dysfunctions, a few rough edges in the central nervous system. But this theory explains too little.

Have they not perhaps, with their genetic code, been born into the wrong nest, where, unintentionally, they are continually called to do what is for them impossible? Have they perhaps an exceptionally sensitive heart? It is conceivable, but it remains exceptionally difficult for the parents, who spend the rest of their lives blaming themselves and asking themselves where they went wrong. Would they take it on my authority that whoever simply shows their child love can never be to blame?

The Cunning Heart

An important question in this connection is whether one, *in the final analysis,* can trust one's heart. "After all, when it comes right down to it, you have to do what your heart tells you to," we often say. Is that good advice?

From the above it should be clear that to a great extent I think it is. But not entirely.

It depends above all on the upbringing. Those who intend to look deep into themselves for advice often run up against deeply rooted prejudices and mistake them for the voice of the heart. A certain healthy skepticism is therefore necessary regarding one's own deep motives.

Love is an experience and a decided devotion. If the latter is not clearly present, love does not last long. Those who love make a decision.

But not entirely. We cannot love anyone and everyone, no matter how much we might like to, under certain circumstances.

Experience may not be denied. The senses may not be denied (the erotic, Chapter 6); the ego may not be denied (the narcissistic, Chapter 7); and the heart may not be denied (the shulamithic, Chapter 8).

We can easily imagine whatever we please. If we desperately want to love someone, we can convince ourselves that in our hearts we are in love. The beautiful hostess from *Im Weiszen Rossl* says at one point, "O well, since I can't get the man that I love, I will just have to love the man I can get." In light of my opinion that love is always mutual, I would say, "Be careful, little girl. The cunning heart allows itself to be blinded for a time, but over the long haul it cannot be coerced. The senses and the ego permit it even less."

Vincent

"I feel it so much in my heart," Vincent said sincerely. He and his wife had come to me in order to talk about their marriage problems. He loves so many of his female friends so much that he sleeps with them on a regular basis if that is where it leads. He calls it "neighborly love," and in his heart he is convinced that he is in the right.

But his wife is not.

"Neighborly love?" I ask, "Are any of them ugly?"

No they are not; they are, oddly enough, all shapely, lovely women. But he thinks it is all so sad, since they either have no one or the one they have does not satisfy them, at least not like he does.

"Do the women know about each other?"

"Actually they don't, no."

"Then you know nothing of the cunning of the human heart."

25

No, he knows nothing of it, nor does he care to. Because "if you can't trust your own heart, who can you trust?"

Vincent's error is that he — with an appeal to the heart — declares himself autonomous and refuses to test his motives and actions against those of others, especially those of the One who is Love.

Testing is not, to be sure, the same thing as merely submitting or adapting oneself to the opinions of others, but neither is it simply vindicating oneself with the help of some flimsy theory constructed to fit the circumstances. There is much popular philosophical nonsense adduced, primarily — but not exclusively — by men, for just such a purpose. What they want is a good roll in the hay and then to lay aside all the precious promises and good intentions and walk away. In the meantime, however, they very seriously, or just loudly, aver that they are concerned with a better world, with the struggle against egoism and smug complacence. That is not testing, just self-deception.

Vincent is not the only one who talks like this. Untouchable and sovereign, he looks down on his wife, who looks to me for help.

I am unable to do anything for her. We will return to Vincent when we deal with the Phoenix.

Heartless

There are a number of people — mostly men — wandering about in Western civilization that appear to have no heart. Of course they do have a heart somewhere — or else they would simply fall to pieces — but they do not know where it is and cannot seem to find it.

Once in a while, when they become aware of it, they make an attempt to find their heart, but they soon give up, since they have no clue as to where it might be or where they should begin to look. It is not because their heart is inaccessible, or protected by armor, but rather because it lies in a distant and neglected, undeveloped part of their self-consciousness. It is a part of them that they simply have never found.

For them the heart is the blood pump. The heart referred to in poems is simply a superfluous, romantic metaphor. "Come on, honey, don't talk nonsense."

26

Apparently this is possible. Apparently people can have a limited self-consciousness and yet (or perhaps therefore) go a long way socially. But in the Land of Love they run amuck, especially if they desire someone who is in touch with her heart.

Darling, What More Do You Want?

Anne (38), two healthy children, married to Thomas (40), a chemist with a high position and a salary to match, hardworking, athletic, very obliging and gallant, nonsmoker, and a very moderate drinker, always ready to do what needs to be done around the house, never looks at other women, very supportive, all she needs to do is glance at something — and she often does because she was raised in the lap of luxury — and he buys it for her.

What a man! Her friends are green with envy. What more could she want?

He also wants her to have her own life. He handles things very well if there is a difference of opinion — he listens attentively, responds to her arguments, and very nobly admits when he is wrong.

And yet something is amiss with their love. She is "happy, but not satisfied."

Everyone is furious: "That ungrateful bitch!"

She tries to explain it to me. "There is nothing wrong with Thomas, but . . ."

"Do you love him?"

"Yes, of course, I think so, I want to, but I just can't seem to. When it comes right down to it, we are like strangers to each other. There is no electricity between us. We never really talk; it is all so superficial and distant. He cares nothing for the things that move me. *We never experience anything together that has any depth;* not sex, not books, not music, not art, not nature — nothing. Not even the kids, really. If I am upset about something, he begins to reason with me and then I lose it. And then I lose him.

"And if you were to tell him this in a quiet moment?"

"He looks at me with big eyes and says that he hasn't any idea what I am talking about. And you know, I think he's right.

27

He says that I am just a sentimental scatterbrain and that thankfully he isn't, because you don't get very far in the world of chemistry like that."

Access to the Heart

There are two aspects of self-consciousness. One does not reach or nourish the heart; the other one does. Pascal calls them "l'esprit de géometrie" and "l'esprit de finesse." What exactly he means by that has been extensively explored, and the opinions differ.

I describe these two aspects in my own way and call them the *technical* and the *open* modes of self-consciousness. *They belong together like the left and the right hand.* But in our Western upbringing and educational system, the technical aspect is strongly emphasized at the expense of the open aspect. As a result, many people walk around with a withered hand, so to speak. Anne's husband, Thomas, is one of them. And her then? That remains to be seen.

The technical aspect of the self-consciousness involves standing at a *cool distance.* It is concerned with explanation and analysis, objectivity, logic, cause and effect, profitability, performance, size and number, "geometry." In short, we are dealing with the positivistic, empirical way of interacting with reality that leads to rational control. Hence the word "technical," which does not refer exclusively to machines. Art historians, for example, and pedagogues and theologians can also interact in a technical way. The emphasis on the technical in upbringing and education has offered us in the West, materially speaking, a great deal of independence.

The open aspect is not so much a question of control, but of *experience.* Not standing at a distance, but *warm proximity,* intimacy, depth, immersion, surrender. Not explanation but stories, which lose their power when they are taken apart and analyzed. It is the revelation of mysteries that lie hidden beneath the empirically observable surface.

The technical aspect breaks water down into its constituent parts: H_2O, freezes at 0° C, boils at 100° C, etc. *But what the true nature of water is can only be experienced through openness.* Openness is never technically very precise. According to the open aspect, for example, water is the "cool drink from the fountain of your love."

We are dealing here not with the parts, but with the whole; not with logic, but with wonder and "finesse"; not with objective observations, but with subjective, harmonious awareness.

Looking Deeply

We must teach our children (and ourselves) to use the senses in both ways. The technical aspect receives much attention and there is a considerable amount of practical material developed for it.

Exercises in perception teach them gradually to sharpen their focus, to discover and distinguish the primary from the secondary, and function from causality. They teach them to "look carefully"; essential for their self-consciousness. But there are other forms of "looking" — looking at the starry skies, a raindrop that runs across the windowpane, a feather lying on the balcony, a picture in a book. Here we encourage the child to let what he has seen impress itself on him, so that he can become aware of the true nature lying hidden beneath the surface. "Hold your breath for a moment, *don't think about anything,* just look, *look deeply.* You will see more than your eyes can see. Then perhaps you will discover a little of the true nature, then you see the *wonder* of it all, and who you really are. There, deep under the surface."

In this same way the child must learn to touch, smell, taste, and hear. This type of exercise of the senses is of highest importance for the erotic, just to give one example.

Those who are unable to look deeply into their hearts never find satisfaction with day to day things. *If the wonder of the true nature remains hidden under the surface, none of the erotic or social skills one has learned or discovered contribute anything to love.* Because the light of hope that the Great Love will be realized is only kindled in those who catch a glimpse of the wonder of it all from time to time. Thus hope counteracts the defensive reactions that clog up the heart. We will return to this in detail below.

Only through the *depth* of the openness of the self-consciousness can the heart be reached, opened, and nourished, so that it can be engaged and applied. "Supra. All systems go. Full capacity. Complete integration."

It now seems evident that men like Thomas have simply never nourished their hearts. That is why it appears that they have no heart.

29

It has remained undeveloped. Their self-consciousness (and therefore their reality-consciousness) is therefore very limited. Water for them is just H_2O, nothing else. Wonderful people, often. Not a thing you can say against them. But in religion, love, and art they are lopsidedly "technical" in their perception and therefore out of touch. Sometimes to a greater, sometimes to a lesser extent. It seems as though they have been split down the middle and have lost a part of themselves. They are not unusual in Western society. The technical aspect of the self-consciousness receives all the attention, even in religious and literary instruction.

With openness, on the other hand, we are all more or less left to our own devices. Some succeed, others do not. Women have an advantage where this is concerned, since they have been, to a certain extent, locked out of the technical in this male-dominated society. This has placed them at a great disadvantage in terms of their ability to control, but it has also had advantages. They have been able to pass on from generation to generation experiences that have remained hidden to men, who are too busy controlling.

What should I say, then, to Anne?

In my opinion, we are not dealing here with the "feminine" and the "masculine," or the "Eastern" and the "Western," as mutual opposites, something along the line of Yin and Yang, or the Anima and the Animus. Nor are we dealing with the opposition between the *vita activa* and the *vita contemplativa* — the working and the contemplative life. And it certainly has nothing to do with the opposition between intellect and emotion.

The two aspects of the self-consciousness are related to each other as the right and the left hand (in which the thumbs work in opposition to the fingers). A person can be predominantly right- or left-handed, but he still needs two good hands. Especially in love, which is experience and devotion. The full self-consciousness is "bi-modal": two-handed.

An Aside

In the East there are many one-handed people. There they are sometimes so utterly open that they serenely smile while allowing the god's water to flow over the god's land rather than using technology to do something about it. The sad part of this one-

30

handedness is that it is not the god's land at all, but belongs to some dirt-poor farmer, who has just lost everything for the umpteenth time and must now sell his daughter in order to survive.

When I raised this point in an ashram in Uttar Pradesh, a well-to-do man answered that the greatness of India was the tremendous capacity the people had for suffering. He thought it tremendous; I did not.

A woman in the village told me I was right. "Our men must get to work. They must think of something so that the dike doesn't break every year. You people in Holland know all there is to know about such things, don't you? Why don't you say something to our men?"

What they have too much of there in that village, we have too little of here.

Together with Anne I had to see whether she is not also sometimes one-handed. She did not think so, and I agreed with her.

What to Do?

In a traditional society dominated by technical men, dependent women generally give up *hope,* and that is one of the worst things a person can do.

"Well, men are just like that."

Did my aunts also belong to this group? My mother certainly did not, of that I am certain.

As a result of our changed circumstances, some women have become sufficiently independent and rebellious to give up their marriages.

"I won't pretend."

Anne says that too. Thomas has not a clue where to begin. He is completely at loose ends because I will not just forcefully call her to *order.* And his female acquaintances, who have already given up hope, are for that same reason deeply disappointed in me.

"Very unchristian of you, Wim."

Those are the words of people who do not believe a bit of it and have left the church far behind. They have not taken the time to keep up on the latest developments in the church. And yet they see the "order" accepted by Anne and Thomas, whether they like it or not, as Christian. Will we never get beyond the miserable Constantinian era?

Call her to order, give up hope, give up the marriage. Is there no other way? Some way to make up for lost ground?

It is possible, but it would have to be together. When Thomas discovers that he has a heart, he will not have a clue what to do with it at first, just like everyone else. And Anne may find him a bit strange at first as well. Thomas could very well make some irrevocable decision and leave her in a lurch. That often occurs with men, when in mid-life, for example, they suddenly discover that they have never really developed whole parts of their selves.

Together then, hand in hand, without feelings of superiority or inferiority in either one. Also no trendy jibes, like, "Thomas should be in therapy!" He should certainly not be in therapy, because he is not sick. He must begin the adventure of the *Queeste*, a journey into new possibilities for himself.

Anne must take him by the hand as a priestess, in order to introduce him to the mysteries of the reality that have, until now, remained hidden for him. They might need an experienced advisor as well, to whom they can explain from time to time how things are going, because those who themselves form part of the problem can so quickly overlook something important. But more than anything they need *time*, and therefore must arrange their schedules differently. Things cannot simply go on as they were before. They also need *rest* and *quiet*. Moreover, Thomas must *entrust* himself to his wife, and she must not abuse this trust.

Is their marriage worth this to them? Do they want this, are they able? (The answer was in this case, sadly enough, no.)

Just one final question for Anne: "Why did you marry him? It is not like you were still some naive kid. Surely you saw it coming?" What follows is a long response, with key words like "nice, good-looking, polite, important, gentleman; a real honor to be asked by someone like that; very skilled in bed; good home environment, high position, top salary; my mother thought he was great."

"But what did you feel? In your heart and his? Did you ever ask, 'Can I do this; do I want this?'"

"I always thought it would come later."

Was she really so naive? Or was she compelled by his technical abilities and top salary?

Hard

In this chapter we have made several claims, which all come down to the fact that there are people who are not *able* to love, because there is something wrong with their heart.

What should be done with them? They all have their attractive, fun, friendly, and even sometimes lovely characteristics.

Almost all of them seek some kind of happiness, and desire to have someone by their side in whom they will find it in some special way. And yet it does not happen, or not for very long. Then they try again, and again. And so they leave behind them a trail of sadness and bitterness, bewildered and saddled with uncertainty and feelings of guilt — both child and adult.

Where should we begin with such people? Be careful: that is the message for them. Do not just recklessly get involved. Think first: "Do I choose this? Am I able? Do I want this?"

But does not love conquer all? Of course, of course, I do not deny it. But love is mutual, as we will clearly show. For people without hope, with a heart that is wrapped in the armor of aversion and bitterness as a result of early childhood (relative) neglect, the offer of love conquers nothing, nor does sex.

Those who want love, with their heart and soul, are compelled to run away if such a person comes near. These people cannot handle anything other than a more or less distant partner-relationship with clear, watertight agreements. Then the only question is how long it will last, because they always want to justify their lifestyle. If anyone rubs them the wrong way — in whatever way — it all goes wrong, in spite of all their charm and other fine qualities. The thought "I'll get through it; it will work out," is often understandable, but always wrong.

There is no moral objection that can be leveled against more or less distant partner-relationships, but if either one of them really desires love, it is very difficult and in the long run unbearable.

With people who appear to have *no heart*, like Thomas, it is often possible to begin somewhere. But it is and remains very difficult, and it always remains to be seen how it will turn out. Those who desire love with heart and soul must be very clear about this. "Will I change him?" It is not impossible, but . . .

For people with *dressaten* — the stereotypical defensive reactions that like clogs can hinder access to the heart — the possibilities are much greater. Some of them are in this regard, however, very intricate and complicated, full of conflicting vulnerabilities. If the defensive reactions develop at an early age, they will not so easily disappear. If they become a hindrance already early in a relationship, one must be careful, because they tend to become ever more cumbersome with time.

But not everyone considers them a burden. Some say, "That is just who I am." Others even say, "I like it. It is precisely what makes her so charming." If that is the case early on, there is no danger.

If the defense mechanisms arise immediately before, during, or after puberty, things are somewhat easier. Through love they can then find that it is not at all necessary to react stereotypically, especially not if the partner makes some effort to avoid the vulnerable places. We will return to this subject in Chapter 7, "Narcissus."

4. *The Phoenix Is Self-Sufficient*

The Wonder Bird Has Returned

In earlier times, out of distant and at that time still mysterious Arabia, there occasionally appeared a miraculous bird. The bird descended on the Egyptian city of Heliopolis, and alighted on an altar in the temple of the god Re.

It was the Phoenix.

The creature appeared but once in five hundred years, as members of the ancient world knew. (Others claimed that it was once every 1,461 years.) It was at the same time beautiful and terrible; the figure of a powerful eagle with crimson feathers. It was neither male nor female and yet was both; it needed no one and nothing; it was self-sufficient. When it sensed that its end was approaching, it burned itself on a nest of spices, *in order, thereafter, to rise anew from the flames and ashes.* (That is why it needed the spices, but we will come back to that.)

Many stories have been told and countless attempts made to depict the Phoenix. The most recent that I know of — and not the worst by far — is that of Marten Toonder.[1]

The Phoenix became a symbol in many different religions. The ancient Christians, for example, saw in the bird something of the resurrection on the Last Day. Now the creature has returned. Without a doubt. The 1,461 years are certainly past.

It has descended on the Land of Love.

1. See Marten Toonder, "De feunix" [The phoenix]. In *Een heer moet alles alleen doen* [A gentleman must do everything alone] (Amsterdam, 1973).

In the meantime the creature has changed. It has become even more autonomous. And more importantly, it has picked something up along the way and taken it up into itself. Indeed, mention was already made of it in the old tales: "An egg of myrrh," they would say, "in the corpse of the father!"

The nature of this egg makes it very important to us now: it is a monad, spherical, and externally closed — a symbol of humankind's relationship to reality.

Androgyny

About four hundred years before Christ, the Greeks were already analyzing love. Plato describes a conversation carried on by a number of wealthy, intellectual noblemen during a drinking party or symposium.

He permits a certain Aristophanes to speak. The man is known as a mediocre writer of comedies. He has the hiccups because he has drunk too much. But after a sneezing fit he feels better and proceeds to explain how love (or better said, eroticism) came about. Originally people were combined beings. Male/males, female/females, and also male/females. The last are called *androgynes,* from the Greek. These combined beings all had two heads, four arms, and four legs.

Everyone laughs. That Aristophanes — what a card!

But these combined beings suffered from "hubris," or pride. They did not know their place in relation to the gods. As punishment, they were cut in two, and since then each piece has sought its other half (its "symbol," as Aristophanes calls it) to which he or she originally belonged, and to which he or she is drawn. That longing is eroticism or love; we will leave open both possibilities for now. (Hence the expression "my better half" to refer to one's partner.)

Again everyone laughs. Well said, Aristophanes!

"And now let us be sure that we do not suffer from hubris, or else we will again be cut in half and will lose a part of ourselves," says the joker, joining the laughter. He is not taken very seriously. (And yet that cutting in two appears to have happened to all those one-handed people.)

What has the strange bird picked up from the tale of Aristophanes during its wanderings?

Not the thought that the erotic desire that people have for each other is a means of recovering their original condition; that lovers are symbols of each other. Sometimes male/males, sometimes female/females, and sometimes male/females and vice versa. Not the thought that the mystery of love can only be discovered if the two pieces of the symbol are joined together once again. The bird did not pick this up.

Nor the idea that we are in danger of being cut in two again if we don't respect the gods. All these ideas were passed over.

The Phoenix has, however, carefully picked up the image of the androgynous being from Aristophanes' story. Actually, that was to be expected. The fabled bird and the androgyne are both *self-sufficient.* They do not need each other, the other, or The Other, in order to be fully themselves and to renew themselves. (If the spices are left out of the picture.)

All of reality is present in their enclosed, spherical Yin and Yang existence. Way down deep, the man is a woman and the woman a man. Even deeper resides the wisdom of all the ages, and beyond that they are all god. The modern Phoenix people arrive at their destination by allowing these deep mysteries to penetrate their being and integrating them into themselves.

And again, they are their own destination. They are indeed cut in two, but the other side is still securely attached, albeit temporarily out of order. That is what they want. Their own, temporarily-out-of-order, other side.

There are other creatures on earth, animals, plants, and things too, but *none of them are the other to which they are drawn.* A person is not among the creaturely, according to them. The other is not part of the destination.

It is certainly not my favorite animal, this modern Phoenix, this androgynous, self-contained, self-sufficient being. I can, however, feel its power of attraction. It is very appealing for people who are lonely and incapable of reaching anyone or anything not to need anything or anyone. There are quite a few of them in our technically inclined society. Anyone who ponders the waves of hate, fear, and pollution that have swept over our world in the last century can only sympathize with those who close themselves up in a Phoenix-like existence. It is sometimes more bearable to be self-sufficient than to love. If it comes to that, they can simply close the blinds of their space capsule and exist all by themselves, apart from the other, elliptically moving within the perfect structures of the harmony of the spheres.

But I cannot. Not at all. It occurs to me that Phoenix people have collectively placed a shield around their hearts out of dissatisfaction with, and fear of, reality. "L'enfer, c'est l'autre" is perhaps their experience: "the other is hell."[2]

How do they fare in matters of love?

Here we have Vincent again, whom I found to have a cunning heart, but who sincerely believes himself to be in the right. His wife can be nothing more for him than a good partner, with whom he has a relationship based on explicit or implicit agreements. He will abide by them, but she must not rub him the wrong way. Actually he does not need her, autonomous as he is. Dwelling together and living together, eroticism and conversations about their own inner experiences; all that is permissible. "But why be exclusive?" he asks. We all have everything within us. What makes one so different from the other?

Vincent cannot bear that people actually "claim" each other. That alienates them from their true, deep self. (Besides, it alienates him from the shapely women.) His wife digs in. She does not want to live like two separate people. If that is the case, they are not really married, in her eyes.

That hurts him, and he hopes that some day she will come as far as he has.

What should I say to her? "He is self-sufficient, because he is under the spell of the modern version of the Phoenix."

"There is not a lot I can do with that," she says, "but at least I understand that I am not just backwards or old-fashioned."

"The age of the Phoenix is almost over. The miraculous creature will soon return to that distant, unknown land that was earlier known as Arabia. Then it will be at rest for five hundred or 1,461 years."

That is what I claim on occasion.

2. These are the oft-quoted words of Sartre from *Huis Clos* (Paris, 1945), translated by Stuart Gilbert as *In Camera* in *Two Plays* (London: H. Hamilton, 1946).

5. Clear-Obscure

Somber Is the Key

Until now ours has been a somber tale, I think. Misunderstandings, problems, and pitfalls. Is love always like that?

It began with the young man in the white jacket, and thereafter followed a colorful, or rather a motley procession of characters who wanted nothing more to do with love, were not to be trusted, or had ended up in misery on account of love. They circulated among the gloomy props of spells, hexes, power, inaccessibility, neglect, heartlessness, cunning, detachment, and isolation. Above this scenario there hovered from time to time an uninspiring predatory bird calling out a dire "Woe, woe," over love.

But the play of love is not at all like that. In fact, the opposite is true!

Why, then, have I written with such a heavy hand? Because love has dangerous and bitter sides, without a doubt. But that does not explain everything.

Why did I start this way? There are many answers to that question.

First, one does such things in order to be taken seriously as an agent of change. Whoever wants to change things for the better must first establish a situation of need and with carefully selected words explain why things cannot continue as they are. If one neglects this task, one cannot expect that attention will be paid to the solutions proposed.

There is another, secondary reason.

In our culture we generally regard optimists as airheads. (Making light of them is condoned; a form of socially acceptable gloominess.) The Greeks were bound by the tragic — the experience that evil can arise from our struggle for the good — and by the already mentioned hubris, pride that oversteps the bounds established by the gods for every human (*moira*). The *joy* of love had little chance to be fleshed out by observers and storytellers.

The later Roman Stoics were even less carefree as lovers, not to mention the Church Fathers and the Stylites. Pessimism made traditional wisdom cynical. That is why Aristophanes was always considered second-rate. His ideas about the combined beings were not so crazy, but he presented them much too lightly.

If that was true of the fun-loving, wine-drinking Greeks under the abundant sun of Attica, and for the Romans in Bella Italia, how much more true for us — somber, beer-sipping Germanics under the low, cloudy skies of the coastal bogs.

Even Levinas

Not only agents of change, but almost all observers write somber tales of love. (Julia Kristeva is a fortunate exception.) Observers explore the boundaries, the shadow side of things. That is why they are interested in the failures. They are hard to make light of, and that sets the tone. Even Levinas is dead serious.

Emmanuel Levinas, a philosopher of Polish-Jewish descent residing in Paris, is, in my opinion, one of the wisest and most important thinkers of our day. He has again made love a matter of inquiry, treating it as something with its own existence, derived from nothing else. That is quite a claim.

Yet he deals with it in a very somber and joyless way. It almost seems that we are condemned to love, and that we bear it as a nearly unbearable burden. A phrase like "He who loves must first learn to accept that it is not himself he loves"[1] does not have a happy ring to it. This expression — which can be traced back to Plato — is not in itself incorrect, because love is not just a transaction. A lover demands no payment for services rendered. That is prostitution.

"True love does not cost anything," Levinas means to say. That

1. In *Otherwise Than Being: or, Beyond Essence,* trans. Alphonso Lingis (Norwell, Mass.: Kluwer, 1981).

sounds much happier, but one apparently cannot or should not speak in this way. Agents of change and observers are, therefore, hardly interested in the positive side of love. And what about the storytellers?

Famous Couples

My father did not enjoy romantic movies. Before the war, my mother liked to go to the movies once a week, but she preferred not to go alone, since she found it to be less cozy. Usually one of her friends went along, since we had won free tickets as a door-prize. As a small child I was also regularly taken along, but sometimes the film was too "realistic." If no one else was available, my father had to fill in.

He was not cut out for it. He only looked at the newsreel and the first five minutes of the film. Then he would turn and say to my mother, "I've already seen this one. First they go through a lot of misery and then the guy with the mustache gets the girl with the long legs. Just wake me up when it's over." Then he would close his eyes. My mother did not mind. Much later, with the advent of television, my father still did not like to watch romantic movies. They were too predictable for him, no matter how much they had changed. The misery was the same; it was still dumped out in bucketfuls.

"First I could predict who would get whom. Then I could predict who would *not* get whom. And now it is clear after five minutes who, at the end of an hour and a half of worry and complications, will *get rid of* whom. That's not the way it goes in real life, is it, Son?"

"Sometimes it is, Dad."

"Sometimes, sometimes. But in those lousy films it is a foregone conclusion. Why would they want to do that? Don't those movie people know what love really is?"

Orpheus and Eurydice are among the oldest, greatest lovers of whom we have knowledge. Location: Thrace, in pre-historical Greece. He plays beautifully on his lyre and sings so wonderfully that not only

41

people, but also animals, plants, and other things are moved. Including the gods.

We would have never heard of their love if misery had not struck. Eurydice is bitten by a snake and descends into the underworld. Orpheus cannot accept that. He goes after her and is able, by means of his music, to win over the divine Persephone so that she permits Orpheus to take his love back with him to the land of the living. But he must promise not to look at her as long as they are in the underworld. Things do not go well, and he returns alone.

The story has been sung in every key, told and retold in every imaginable way.

It is truly a profound story, and very moving. But it is not a true myth: it does not reveal the truth. Not in my opinion.

Tristan and Isolde, an old British tale, also has been told in every which way. Wagner made it into a famous musical drama. Terribly German!

Tristan and Isolde love each other, but they are unable to have each other, at least not for long.

She is a lovely Irish princess, who is won, with much difficulty, by the noble Tristan. Unfortunately not for himself, but for his uncle Marc, king of Cornwall. During the journey to Cornwall they drink the "drink of love," and die the "death of love." Now what is that, the death of love? The *life* of love seems so much more important to me, but we do not find it in this story.

Romeo and Juliet. Perhaps these are the most famous lovers in world literature. Completely crazy about each other, but here too things go awry. The politics of Verona come between them. Death and destruction! The lovers come from two feuding families. Then the church, in the person of the naive brother Lorenzo, attempts to devise a ruse, but that too goes awry. These lovers are also "united in death."

"For never was a story of more woe / than this of Juliet and her Romeo," Shakespeare somberly comments at the end of the play through the character of the Prince. A stage direction follows in brackets: "[All exit]."[2]

Never? What about Hamlet and Ophelia, Anthony and Cleopatra?

Nevertheless, death does not unite. Life can unite, but death separates. Greedy Thanatos, the god of the dead, has never once united lovers. The

2. *Romeo and Juliet,* V.iii.309-10.

trials, the suffering, the failures, and the deed are described in great detail in the tales of love. You see, storytellers must relate the exceptional, the dramatic, and the pathetic. No one from any cultural level listens, looks, or reads if he or she simply imitates normal, everyday life. For example, Stendhal, Flaubert, Ibsen, Proust, and Baudelaire, just to pick a few names out of the hat. The list could easily be lengthened, for example, with Russians! Exceptionally dramatic misery from the lot of them!

Even in fairy tales it is often all so very difficult, even though after the many trials and tribulations they always end with "and they lived happily ever after." But you seldom if ever read how it is in real *life*.

Clear-Obscure

Agents of change, observers, and storytellers are therefore not interested in true, commonplace love. But perhaps we can still do something with their insights.

In order to do so we must borrow an old artists' technique, going back to Da Vinci and Correggio: the *chiaroscuro*, the "clear-obscure."

These artists discovered that if they wanted the light to appear brighter in their paintings, drawings, or wood carvings, they had to take care to make sure that the *dark aspects* of the painting were highlighted. The technique introduced by them runs through Rembrandt; who is, in my opinion, the best example. But there are many more.

Perhaps it is also true with the subject of love that through the "obscure," through the darkness of spells and hexes and delusions and irrationality, fate, death, lifelessness, and loss . . . that precisely through the obscure the "clear" of love becomes brighter.

That is certainly not the effect intended by all the gloom-and-doomers, because there are many among them who are simply without hope. But Levinas may have intended it that way. At least I hope so.

(Light can be depicted in other ways as well, as has been amply proven by the Impressionists, the best example being, in my opinion, Van Gogh. They hardly needed "obscure" and dared to depict the "clear" of the sun and flowers directly. Artists have always known what to do with the "clear" of love; as the cover of this book clearly demonstrates. Composers and poets traditionally have been and are able to do a great deal with it as well.)

43

Although we too belong to the (observing) agents of change, we will attempt from now on to take a different tack than they did. From now on the obscure will only enter tangentially. For it seems to me that there is already enough talk about the dark sides of love. We know they are there. Earlier we, too, took the wrong path in the Land of Love. We ended up in the dark regions. If we continue along that same path we will never see what the true possibilities are.

Clear

The wonder of love, with all its joys, fullness, ecstasies, and mysteries, is found in day-to-day living. There — in daily discourse; for better or for worse, in the peaks and plains and valleys and canyons; for richer or for poorer, in sickness and in health, till death do us part — there, and nowhere else, true love takes shape.

There is everything that we long for: enjoyment, pleasure, and joy; hiddenness and insight; eating and drinking; the power to live and die; comfort in suffering; light of the sun, moon, and stars; self-realization; the dewdrop of existence; harps and angel songs; a fire in the cold and coolness in the heat; the final answer to the "Why?" of longing for fulfillment, happiness, "foretaste."

How can there be love? What is love? What can we *do* in order to experience it?

These are important questions, because the above emotionally ecstatic description still falls short of the mark. After all, I am no poet. We will attempt in this and the following chapters to find an answer, in order to return to it again later in another connection.

We would do well here to remember the modest pretensions of this book. *Something,* we stated in the first chapter — we want to clarify *something* of the wonder. More than that is not possible.

Being Other Makes Love Possible and Necessary

"Don't ask how, just take advantage of it!" runs the rather worn slogan of merchants with unbelievable bargains. Those who are satisfied with such a slogan where love is concerned have my sympathy. I have my own thoughts on the subject. Perhaps they will help us answer the question regarding what we can do to experience love.

It is possible; love is possible, because people understand what it means to *be other* in relationships. That is one of my central thoughts.

Ontic Experiences

Everyone has memories of great and small ontic experiences. I can still see, smell, and taste the mound of red sand in front of our flower shop when they laid the sewer in our village. It ran through my fingers, and when my mother brought me water I was able to shape it, although not entirely as I wished. The red sand also had something to say about it. Together we sought— the other and I — what was and was not possible.

And suddenly there was something on top of me, pressing my face into the sand. I can still taste it, together with the blood from a split lip. I am suffocating, but then there is air and the mother of the enormous retarded boy from the next street pulls me, sobbing, up by the arm. "Now, now, Wimmie. Jan just wanted to play with you."

Gasping, I pull the life and breath back into me. Later they tell me that I even smiled and gave Jan a bloody, snotty sand-kiss. But now I believe that it was not only out of friendliness that I smiled at Jan, but out of an understanding of what it means to be other, that which constitutes our self-consciousness and re-ality-consciousness.

What else? The free, shiver-inducing pleasure of the water around me when I first experienced the primitive swimming pool — taken along by a friend of my mother and complete with bathing cap in order to pass as a girl, because in those days coed swimming was still prohibited.

Idly eating an abundance of pears in the sun under the great tree.

The sun over the hay fields; the tough stems and strange smells of the flowers in the flower shop; Frits, the neighbor's horse, who good-naturedly let me drive him in front of the grocer's cart; Jetta, a blond girl whom I never met but who in

45

my sixth year made it known to me via a friend that she would like to walk with me. Ha! My grandfather's white goat and the strange taste of its warm, fresh milk; the starry skies during the war, with the drone of passing aircraft.

In addition to these there are suddenly countless clear memories of *experiences of being and therefore of being other.*

This type of open experience of reality (all systems go and full speed ahead), these so-called "ontic experiences," are among the most essential that I can imagine.

For that reason I cannot get around existence — my own, that of the other and others — not even if I wanted to. The other and others "impress themselves upon me as such" with their own nature and their own needs and questions. Sometimes with outspoken words, more often with unspoken words. Levinas speaks here of the "face of the other."[3]

Now I have come to another central thought: *the other and others ask something of me. They want to be dealt with in accordance with their nature. They seek an answer, hold me responsible, and therefore make me free.*

Since I am other than the other and others, I can love; I can assume my position in reality "dialogically" — as one who questions and answers. Open to and related to the other and others.

Allow others to "impress themselves upon me," as Levinas states it, but that is too obscure for me. The other and others *are there for me and I for them.* As a gift — and therefore also as a duty, but I want to emphasize the gift at this point.[4]

We should not exist without each other. As a creature I am related to them — to others through my heart, to the animals through my consciousness, to the plants and other things through my corporeality. Because I am other, *I am not on my own,* not directed toward myself, not simply thrown down somewhere.[5]

Because I am other, *I may be* free, responsible, dialogical. The other

3. In *Existence and Existents* (The Hague, 1978), among others.

4. There is a close relation between the Dutch words *gave* (gift) and *opgave* (duty) that cannot be expressed in translation. — *Trans.*

5. This is a play on a well-known idea of Heidegger, who several times characterized human existence as *geworfen sein,* that is, "being thrown down"; like a stone that is thrown down here, but could just as well have been thrown down there.

and others welcome my "being-other-in-relationship" in order to be sun and moon for me.

Father Venatius

"Do you realize," Sandra pressed, "that with all that optimistic drivel you place yourself in the company of those wimpy, laughable, naive clowns like Pallieter, Toon Hermans, and Father Venatius?"

I had not yet realized it, but she was right. Go ahead and say "yes" to life, with an "amen" and a "glory hallelujah."

There you have it again, the Aristophanes effect.

"Don't you know," she continued, "that most descriptions of ontic experiences — a far cry better than yours, I might add — disgust me?"

"I know, I know. That happens to me too. I know every nook and cranny of the labyrinth of suffering. But I am about to say something profound again: the memories of my ontic experiences reach forward toward, they anticipate, another experience of reality, which reaches back, or 'retrocipates,' the initial experience. Let me tell you again about the mosaic of Trier. Then it will be clear what I am trying to say, I hope."

"Nicely said, but for the time being the other is a threat to me."

Mutual Respect for Each Other's Nature

It is very important, then, that the other and others *not* invite me to be absorbed into them, to give myself up to them, to identify with them, or to melt into them. Then I would no longer be other and therefore responsible. Then I am of no use to anyone or anything. They must for the same reason not invite me to conquer them or possess them. Or, like a wolf with a lamb, "devour them in love." Then they would no longer be other and the dialogue would dissolve into a monologue.

And if others ask this of me, they do violence to reality. We will have to return to this point repeatedly.

47

They may, however, invite me to love them, that is — as a temporary expression — to make a lifelong pact of mutual respect for each other's nature. A community of dialogue. Then we come — I, the other, and others — into our own right (which we will touch upon again soon). So on the basis of my *ontic experiences* alone I cannot avoid the fact that we are called to love.

Called. It is thus possible for me to avoid the dialogue. I am able to shirk my responsibility. I can deny love. Perhaps I am free enough to give myself up, to attempt to devour the other and others through conquest and annihilation. Perhaps I am not free. Perhaps I have become, through nonexistence or simply through myself, as the old doctrine says, inclined not to love, but to have power over, to hate, to annihilate the other.

That may all be true, *but I cannot get around the ontic experiences.*

Drops from the Primal Sea

I am not familiar with the so-called *oceanic* experience. As an experience of reality, at least, it has never happened to me.

The *ontic* experience is about being *other.* Thereby one becomes a "person." Thereby responsibility, freedom, and love are possible. Yet it is "being-other-in-relationship."

In the oceanic experience the person disappears at the expense of the related. That is experienced by some as nirvana. With me it would sooner provoke a feeling of cosmic angst. In the oceanic experience a person feels himself to be part of an eternal, nameless, great, infinite whole. As a tiny drop of water rising from the primal sea, and destined to return to it again, in order perhaps to rise and return again in an eternal cycle without beginning or end. Love here is the coalescence of drops and the return to the ocean.

There is something very beautiful and familiar about this. All life derives from the ocean. This is the fruitful fluid that surrounds us in the hiddenness of the womb and from which we emerge, sputtering, to the light of day. The same water in which we are baptized. But my recognition goes no farther than this. I, in all honesty, have no idea what to do with the namelessness, the dissolution in eternal cycles. Not in life, not in belief, and absolutely not in love. Symbiosis — meant as the inability to live without each other — is for me a reprehensible attempt at love.

I do not experience myself as an anonymous drop in the primal sea, but I can get very excited about the fact that my *name* is "engraved on God's palm."

That brings us to another experience of reality.

Creator and Creature

There are open experiences of reality that are called "religious experiences." Not everyone arrives at such experiences; especially not in these times. And those who do arrive often do not have a clue as to what to do with them, if an intellectual category in the form of symbols is lacking.

Joachim Wach calls the religious experience "a response to that which is experienced as the ultimate reality."[6]

Ultimate? Perhaps the oceanic experience is more religious than ontic.

It is good to be extremely careful in appealing to these sorts of experiences. They have been and are all too often used as arguments in debates for which, by their very nature, they are completely unsuited. The only thing we can do with them is openly relate them and test them against those of others. The latter is essential, I think. Those who think themselves to have perceived something of The Light and do not want to refine their experiences or share them with others through a system of symbols are like Vincent and his self-sufficient Phoenix.

In the tradition within which I interpret my religious experiences — with its various currents and groups — the religious experience is viewed as a *God-experience*, an encounter with the Holy One. Yet sometimes he is a hidden God, who does not allow himself to be experienced. People who want to believe have always had an extremely difficult time

6. See here the works of J. Wach, *Vergleichende Religionsforschung* [The comparative study of religion] (Stuttgart, 1962); G. Bouritius et al., *Religieuze ervaring: Een veelvormig perspectief op de zin van het bestaan* [Religious experience: A polymorphic perspective on the meaning of existence] (Tilburg, 1988); and A. A. van den Berg, *Als mensen door God worden aangeraakt* [When people are touched by God] (Diss., Brussels, 1988), and their respective bibliographies. In the work of Bouritius et al., see also the complete bibliography of Weima.

with the hiddenness of God. "Why have you forsaken me?" The reality in this tradition is "Creator and creature." The two are not the same.[7] God is the immanent Other and therefore cannot simply be plugged into what we said above by way of introduction to the ontic experience.

The love of and for God is experienced in the Christian tradition as grace. "We can love the Creator and his creation because he first loved us." I am going to skip over the question as to which stories, personal experiences, and other considerations provide the basis for this. That is the task of theology.

But when we acknowledge God, the immanent Other who grants us love, by calling him "Creator" — not so much in the technical as in the open sense — and by calling the world of people, animals, plants, and things "creation," something very important occurs. It becomes possible to make a connection between the God-experience and the ontic experience. They anticipate and "retrocipate" each other, and form together the full reality consciousness (= self-consciousness).

Reality is always, however, qualitatively and quantitatively greater than that which the self-consciousness can contain. That is true both for the whole and for each of its constituent parts. *The nature of reality is not only more than its individual qualities, it is also more than I can experience.* No plant, no animal, no person — nothing is contained in what I can perceive, believe, or imagine. And where God is concerned, that is even more true.

If I love, then the Other, the other, and others remain other, more compelling, more fascinating, more worthy of my love, than I can comprehend. With love we are never finished.

An Aside

For that reason — once again — it is not good to confine the God-experiences in a rational, explanatory, ecclesiastical or

---

7. The terms *creator* and *creature* are a reflection of the work of P. Kohnstamm, whose *Persoonlijkheid in Wording* [Personality in becoming], 3rd ed. (Haarlem, 1959), made a great impact on me at the time. It is, of course, the belief that lurks behind these words that interests me. I am no stone randomly thrown down (see n. 4), but a creature *ex nihilo*, which is not derived from this or that, but free and responsible.

50

nonecclesiastical "doctrine" with the purpose of using it to attack others. The reality of God is always greater and "other" than all the gnostics, mystics, and commentating theologians combined can relate. Communicating ineffable experiences must be done through visions, stories, rituals, and symbols. That is why the early Christians correctly named their confessions "symbols." They chose that term with care because they were aware of what a symbol is: something accessible to us which points to another, still hidden, not yet revealed, mysterious part of reality.

We are never finished with love. But it is not some kind of terrible burden that we must bear with sighing: "Alas, it is always just out of reach."

No need to be somber. Love opens a different perspective on the future. "O happy future that on me shines. . . ."[8] The farther we press on in the Land of Love — assuming that we are on the right path — the more beautiful it becomes. And we have not yet seen the best.

The Mosaic of Trier

Years ago I was present in Trier when a Roman mosaic was uncovered. It was a large and intricate pattern of colorful lines, decorations, and pictures. But not undamaged. There were cracks and gaps visible.

8. Psalm 16:5ff., as versified in the Dutch Psalter:

O blijvooruitzicht dat mij streelt,
ik zal, ontwaakt, uw lof ontvouwen,
U in gerechtighied aanschouwen,
verzadigd met uw godd'lijk beeld

Which, roughly translated, reads:

O happy future that on me shines,
Awake, I will unfurl your praise,
in righteousness upon you gaze,
filled with your heavenly image.

The words seem to be out of date, but all that there is to experience of faith, hope, and love between heaven and earth are summed up for me in these lines.

51

The people who stood around looked at it in different ways. Some only had an eye for the terrible damage that had been done. What they saw was not formed by the pattern of the mosaic, but by the obscure, the *apparent* pattern of cracks and gaps. They did not notice the clear of beautiful colors and the harmonious play of lines. That became clouded in their eyes, until it became something that could be denied. I call that a reality-perception defect.

Others acted as though the brokenness did not exist. It was futile in their eyes.

"Lovely, lovely!"

"What about the gaps and cracks?"

"What gaps and cracks?"

For their own peace of mind they had not even noticed the details. I call that a reality-perception defect too.

The third group was excited about the discovery, but saddened by the brokenness. Nevertheless, they could see past it. They understood that the flaws did not form the pattern of the mosaic. They resolved to *do* something about it, so that the entire mosaic would shimmer and shine in all its beauty and glory once again, just as it was intended.

In a limited way this example can help us.

For those who are willing and able to "see" the true pattern, love is *possible and necessary,* because reality, to which we, in our being other, also belong, is designed for it. Some day the mosaic must and will be restored, shimmering and shining in all its beauty and glory. Love will reveal *true love.*

The ancient question — formulated by Augustine as *Unde Malum?* or "From where does evil (originally) come?" — must be set aside. So long as it is not for too long.

Evil forms no pattern. But it is there. We must not just accept that fact, because it does not belong there. The cracks and gaps are not part of the original creation, but belong to nonlife, to chaos. It must be combatted; *not with hate, but by effective resistance, which is one of the expressions of love.*

Augustus and the Beatles were right. "Ama et fac quod vis" (Love and do what you want), and "All you need is love."

Essential Conditions

Love can be seen — "clearly and distinctly" — as possibility and necessity, as a gift and a duty. It does not allow reality to be reduced to its technical aspects, but seeks to treat everyone and everything according to their own nature. That is the only way to continually renew life.

In order not to wander too far afield with our observations, we will confine our thoughts more specifically to love for and from a beloved.

Above we attempted to bring together a number of so-called *essential conditions,* which partially overlapped with each other. An essential condition is a type of *sine qua non,* a condition that must be met if there is to be a relationship of love.

If the characteristic conditions are not met, we enter into some other kind of human partner relationship. There are many kinds of these. Those who choose them should know that themselves, and they do well not to expect the same thing from their relationship as from a relationship of love.

The first essential condition is that love is a *turning* of the heart, and therefore a turning of the *whole person,* because there is nothing in the heart that is not first in the senses and the ego. The consequences of this for daily life will be discussed in Chapter 6, "Eros," who seeks the sensual; in Chapter 7, "Narcissus," who seeks his ego; and in Chapter 8, "Shulamite," who lies like a seal on her lover's heart.

The second essential condition that we met is derived from the first. In love the *entire self-consciousness* is engaged: the left and the right hand with their opposing thumbs. Both the open, in order to live, and technical, in order to act effectively. Love comes to expression in day-to-day life. It is not just a "warm and good feeling," but a *way of life.* This is worked out in terms of its life application in Chapter 9, on "fundamentals."

The third essential condition that we found was that love is *dialogical* and at its zenith is *osmotic.* That means first of all that we need *two* for love. I and Someone, someone, or *something.* If one of the two disappears — through absorption, coalescence, devouring, surrender, aversion, death, or conquest — love is over.

Second, love maintains a deep *mutual* respect for the nature of the other. It must come from both sides and it must be *equal.* It is question and response, explicitly and implicitly, giving and receiving again (which

53

is different than give and take). It is the willingness to lose oneself in order to find and to be found.

Third, as long as it is not accepted, every offer of love remains desire, longing, yearning in monologue. A person can suffer enormously from this. He or she can become rebellious, depressed, or aggressive. Yet in my opinion the offer of love and the desire for it is in itself not love. *Mutuality is an essential condition.*

Can that really be true?

Rita

I have always wondered whether one who rejects an offer of love is really worthy of love. Love must never be a favor. It does not work that way. It is all or nothing. Perhaps I am being a bit too radical, but take, for example, Rita.

Rita is forty-eight now. She was kept on the line for thirty years (!) by a married man who was ten years her senior. He could not choose her, but he could not turn her away either. And so he let it drag on. It was to his advantage too, since in that way he always had a place to spend the night where he was admired and pampered.

She, from her side, called it love and commitment. She continued to hope that he would one day choose her. In the meantime, for all those years, her heart was locked up, and she did not have the chance to turn it toward another. Why a person does such a thing is often very complicated. When I would tell her that love is mutual and that she would be better off giving that man a good kick in the pants, she would just smile sadly.

"Love is always a sacrifice and that is why it is always one-sided."

"No, Rita, no. How do you figure? That is the excuse of a resigned woman. You cannot sacrifice yourself for some guy who is not worth it. And any guy who is worth it will not ask that you sacrifice yourself. He would say: 'Are you crazy? If there is any sacrificing to be done around here, I will do it!' True love is mutual and goes through thick and thin. But making yourself of no account and humiliating yourself is not part of it, because the loving other will always want you to come into your own right. If he does not, you'd better put an end to it fast.

"Furthermore, that man does not come into his own right through your one-sided, so-called sacrifice. He is simply indulging himself—and that is altogether different."

Now she is animated. Happy. The sadness is gone.

"You call yourself a Christian, right? Then what about Christ's sacrifice? And loving your enemies?"

"Rita, get a grip on yourself! The Lord did that in order to free us from subjection. Not so that the egotists could do whatever was convenient for them.

"I would like to talk again sometime about loving your enemies. But that has nothing to do with what we are talking about here. Besides, I am not saying that you must hate the man. I am saying that you must *resist* the injustice that he is doing you. Thirty years on the line. That is terrible!"

"I am not on the line, and he is not doing me an injustice."

The sadness is back. Did I say the wrong thing? What a misguided understanding of sacrificial love! Or is there more to it than that?

Sacrificial Love

The question is worth repeating. Can we claim that mutuality is an essential condition for love?

Rita's remark about sacrificial love and the love of enemies had nothing to do with her situation. But they cannot simply be set aside. Nor will we set them aside. But first we would like to return to an example that we presented earlier—namely, the love of parents for their children. A parent's love for a child is unconditional, we said, no matter what happens. Is that not in contradiction with what we said about mutuality?

The Woman in the Bathrobe

In the newspaper I read an article about a woman who every day saw a young man riding past on a motorcycle throw his

Suddenly they were very definitely my enemies again — all of them — and the Lord wanted me to love them. I could only accomplish that by quickly leaving our mountain cabin before I punched out their laughing little weasel faces. It was years before I was able to interact with individual Germans again without thinking about that situation, with which they had nothing to do.

Love my enemies. Does that mean that I have to treat them as persons rather than parts of a nameless whole? It is difficult, but it is possible, and I need not surrender my condition of mutuality.

But what about those who have personally impinged upon my life and happiness? What about the one who hates me, who wants to kill me? If I must love him, I will have problems. Perhaps in my better moments it is possible, with the help of the Holy Spirit.

"In his heart, he who hates is deeply unhappy. He holds up to me the mirror of who I could have been. That slap in the face, that was the hand of God, my brother." Such notions have never been foreign to the best of our human race. But then the condition of mutuality must be given up. I can no longer reason my way out of it. Nor do I want to. I must return to those parents who salvage mutuality by investing a great deal in their child with the hope that it will someday be repaid.

But that is another subject.

Covenant

The third essential condition for love was that it must have a covenantal character. This is not just some pact or contract closed by two parties to their mutual advantage, but an eternal *we*-covenant that gives the parties their basic perspective. A covenant. A covenant is based on *mutually entrusting ourselves to each other*.

"I Won't Promise Anything!"

Karl and Lisbeth had lived together for some time, but now they wanted to be married. In fact, they even wanted a church wedding.

But before they could get married, they needed to have a talk with the pastor. Karl just wanted to talk about the ceremony, but the pastor also wanted to talk about love and marriage.

"I would rather not," Karl said, "because then you will start asking questions. And I don't want that because I *won't promise anything!*"

"You won't promise anything??"

"No. I love Lisbeth now, but I cannot promise that I will love her in three years."

That is nonsense. The guy does not love her. He only says that because he has not the slightest idea what it means. She apparently is not the justification for his existence, his everything. He has never gone deep with her, with the senses, the ego, and the heart. There has never been a night where he lay awake listening to the sound of her breathing and thought to himself, "I don't know what life has to offer, but it cannot be more than this moment. Oh my love, you are everything to me. I am not going to sleep. I am going to stay awake the entire night so I can listen to the heavenly music of your breathing."

He has never arrived at such a point, and he may never arrive there in his entire life, in spite of the fact that he passed the course on "Sex and Communication in Partner Relationships." He finds her appealing, exciting, and pleasurable. He admires her endlessly and he loves to be with her. But he wants no *covenant;* he does not want to be bound. He wants out when she begins to bore him. *And she undoubtedly will bore him,* if he is unable to be certain whether he will still love her in three years. He was so convinced that he even reacted violently when someone had the audacity to suggest it to him.

"But statistics show . . ."

"Drop dead. Lisbeth and I are not one of your statistics. Not us!"

Of course it is possible that people who love each other lose each other; to death or to nonlife, and I am not sure which is worse. But a temporary we-covenant? Temporary love? No, that does not exist.

Men like that should not marry. They should look for a woman who thinks that such a partner relationship is sufficient.

And Lisbeth? She is not at all happy about his views, but she makes her peace with them.

The pastor dared not raise an objection. Why not? If I were him I would have grabbed that Karl by the seat of his pants and thrown him out the door and would have yelled after him, "Let me promise you something!"

A loving person has a number of covenants. They surround her like concentric circles, which can be called "we-circles." The larger a circle is, the more people it can include, but the contact will be less frequent and less intimate. Every we-circle must be sustained in its own special way, or the effect weakens.

There is more to be said here that is useful for daily living. We will explore more of this in Chapter 9.

The Other as Such

Those who love deal with the other *as such*. That is, with respect for their true nature. In essence, love cannot be a question of personal gain, convenience, advantage, or profit.

That is a difficult condition, and one that can be posited only because above we so strongly emphasized the mutuality of love.

She Agreed Immediately

We already mentioned it, but it deserves repeating here. Love is not a transaction, not a contract of mutual benefit between partners who see something in each other and try to put it into an agreement.

Such agreements are made, but things get dangerous when noncontractual expectations are attached to them. Sometimes that happens immediately, sometimes over time.

"I thought that the love would come!" or "At first I had no illusions, but then I began to love her. But she didn't love me, and then I was stuck. I wouldn't have left for all the money in the world, but staying was hell, because she would only abide by the agreements we had made."

It can also happen that people begin with such a reasonable contract and that the fire of love suddenly flares up in the two contracting parties and turns them into lovers. But I would not count on it.

It is also possible that the contracting parties continue for the rest of their lives and are reasonably happy.

"This was my thinking: A man alone is really nothing; it is good for business to have a woman at home. I told her that. She agreed immediately. She wanted to have a place of her own too. So we got married and we have never had many problems. For forty years. She is a wonderful wife, good for business, great with the purse strings, and neat and clean. She cooks a great hotdish and you can generally get along with her."

"But do you love her?"

"That's what I said. She is neat and clean and she cooks a great hotdish."

Right.

That was the old way of doing things, but there are countless modern variations. Sometimes things work out very oddly.

For example, a young woman once told me that after a very stormy youth, she felt that she needed to settle down. But she was not sure how or where. One night, after a party, she accompanied a man home. The following morning the sun shone so brightly and he had such a lovely house, such a lovely garden, and such a lovely goat pen with little white goats that she thought, "This is the place!"

He agreed immediately, because he really wanted a relationship again, and the second income was very welcome too, in light of the high mortgage payments. And so . . .

As she relates this to me she is in tears, because he has had *enough* of her now. He has fallen in love with *someone else,* and she has to go.

"Have you fallen in love with him?"

"Well, no. That's not it. I just find it so cruel."

And I just find it so infinitely stupid. Inherent in every contract is the fact that it can be undone when it is no longer mutually beneficial. For that reason every contract should include a conclusion clause.

It is very common that the contracting parties have enough of each other, because contracts have nothing to do with the *other as such*, with their true nature, with their person. They have everything to do with potential for profit. In the case of this man: sex, a second income, intelligent companionship, a couple of extra hands in the garden and the goat pen. So why is she complaining?

If the man were in love he would not be talking about *someone else*. A contractor and a lover cannot be compared.

Certainly not. But who knows what has taken place between these two people in terms of passionate conversation, camaraderie, and intimacy? How often have they pretended that they were lovers? How often have they pretended, in order to get along, that they cared about each other? The fact that they have by such actions made a deposit in an account from which they can never withdraw can leave one with lifelong scars and the other completely cold.

The other as such means nothing, *given her circumstances,* in spite of what the other may represent, do, have, and want.

But certainly not in spite of the past. A person does not have a past, he is his past, in a certain sense. Sometimes the past with a previous lover is not closed; they call it the "past-imperfect tense." All kinds of old understandings and experiences run around loose. And no matter what happens, they attach themselves to the new lover.

Ignoring all this would be irrational — a reality-perception defect — and we have already established that the heart is suprarational.

The other as such means that we do not get involved with just anyone, an attractive *someone* who possesses certain qualities (college education, blond, six feet tall, nice house, lovely garden, and goat lover), but with this particular person.

The other as such means that there is a spark that ignites a fire: "You are my everything, the treasure of my heart, my love!"

All the other blond goat owners with college diplomas, nice houses, and lovely gardens suddenly no longer exist and will never again exist.

"And if your blond hairs turn gray or fall out, and if we have to leave our nice house, garden, and goats and move into the low-rent district, that is fine with me — as long as you are with me. My love, my love, my life."

One's Own Right

What are people looking for when they love each other?

The words "one's own right" have been mentioned a few times. The other must come into his or her own right. It should be clear that the phrase is used here in its visionary sense. If that is too vague, there are other expressions at our disposal: the other must be able to be herself, happy, contented, satisfied. The best that is in her must come to expression. She must achieve her purpose. Her perfection must come to light. She must as much and as often as possible get a "foretaste" of the fulfillment of the Great Longing.

She must shimmer and shine in beauty and glory. Shine as the sun, gleam as the moon. Because she is my sun!

Shimmer and gleam. That is "one's own right," for everyone and everything. Love is the justification of my existence.

I cannot express it better.

Three Mythical Figures

The way in which we practice love in the West is very much influenced by our connection to several mythical figures. By myth I mean here a story that attempts to relate the *truth* about human existence, in this case love.

We already met some of these figures in Chapter 2. There they made an ominous impression. That is why we left them behind when we chose the path of the clear.

We have not yet, however, made the acquaintance of three others, who — perhaps without our knowledge — inevitably play a big role in the way we love. In order to give them their rightful place, we will in the following chapters turn our attention to them. They have already been introduced:

63

Eros, who, when left to himself, *desires* only *something* sensual.

Narcissus, who *longs* only for *someone* (a companion) for his ego.

And *Shulamite,* in whom erotic and ego-love come fully into their own right, in that they *yearn* for their *loved one,* who can turn her heart to them.

6. Eros

Enticing

We all know him: Eros. The ancient god who lent his name to such things as erotica and the erotic. Those are references to sensual love, sensuous and *enticing*. Since the beginning we have, on the one hand, favored him, and on the other, feared him a little.

What does this Eros have to do with true love?

That is a very important question, and one that has occupied us since the dawn of civilization. Many answers have been proposed, varying from "nothing" to "everything." And so we must form our own opinion.

Probably the best-known image of Eros is that which stands in Picadilly Circus, London. There he has the form of a handsomely built, winged young man, armed with a bow and arrow with which he targets unsuspecting passersby so that they get the desire. Sometimes it is wonderful, and sometimes very confusing.

Eros is also known under the Roman name of Amor or Cupido. These Cupids are usually mocking, laughing boys who unexpectedly shoot their little arrows from behind a fold in the curtain or from a branch in a tree. (The *putti* who appear frequently in Renaissance paintings are closely related.)

As far as I know, we find the name Eros for the first time in Hesiod's *Theogony* — the account of the origin of the gods. That was in the eighth century before Christ. Eros was at that time still a powerful god, who brought order to chaos by "uniting the disparate elements." Unfortunately things did not remain that way.

Later he suddenly appears as the son of Ares, the god of war, and Aphrodite, the goddess of fertility and the spring, better known to us by her Roman name, Venus. In the temples dedicated to her, she was worshiped through rituals of sensual love-making with her priestesses (and of course by not forgetting to put something in the offering shell on the way out). Father Ares (his Roman name is Mars) was worshiped by practicing the technique of brutal, ruthless war.

Since then we have often seen the little Eros in the company of his beautiful mother, Venus.

He is already that naughty little arrow shooter. His mother is that eternally enticing beauty, that object of lust, who is at the same time the goddess of fertility. His father is the god of war.

Erotica in these terms is a game for brutal, ruthless (real!) men who make short work of (temple) whores.

In the national museum in Athens there is a beautifully preserved group sculpture of Venus and Eros, along with the god Pan — half man, half goat. He apparently also belongs there, the *pan*ic-causing, horny goat god, with his need for green buds.

Frivolous Sex Object

In the Uffizi, one of the most important museums of Florence, there is a statue that held the world in absolute rapture for a few centuries. It is called the Medici Venus. This dream woman appears to have been a copy of a work by Praxiteles, who lived in the fourth century B.C. Three centuries ago Cosimo III managed to get his hands on this statue and gave her an absolutely perfect place of honor. That is to say, there was and is in the Uffizi a kind of intimate, erotic-esthetic temple — the Tribuna — just perfect in form and dimension. That is where she was placed, and there she stood again. The dream woman, just for Cosimo and his friends. Enticing.

Everyone knows her from thousands of portraits. She is actually very decent. The right hand supports the left breast, the left hand is held more or less over the shameful parts. She is looking slightly off to the left. Nice girl, nothing special, rather frivolous. *I think.*

But what excitement. The masculine, intellectual West went completely crazy. Countless copies, drawings, and engravings were spread over all of Europe and North America. Louis XIV had her copied in bronze because he had to have her nearby. Napoleon could not live without her either. He left all the other art treasures in Florence undisturbed, but the Medici Venus had to go to Paris. It is even said that not long ago a plaster cast of her was held under lock and key in Philadelphia since it was feared that the students would go completely mad over her and would fondle her — and themselves — if they should espy her.

She has, in the meantime, undergone a complete change of appearance. She no longer stands alone in the elitist Tribuna; now she can be found completely democratized in pornographic magazines, advertisements, films, and videos. And so Venus is still today venerated as the dream woman by violent men who want to awaken Eros through her. She herself is not quite so popular anymore. But that's all right. There will always be some who consider lovely, enticing, submissive, and frivolous a great combination.

This erotica fulfills in some way the essential conditions described in the preceding chapter. These myths, however, do not tell the truth about love. *This Eros leads to whores and violent men from the dark side of the land of love.*

The answer to the question of what erotica has to do with true love is therefore now in order. You might be saying, "As far as I am concerned, it shouldn't be that way!" I agree, but are there perhaps other ways? The early Christian church could hardly be anything but radical in her response. The temples of Venus were destroyed and replaced with churches and convents. The temple whores were sent home, and quietistic, ascetic monks took their place. They were unable to answer the question of the place and worth of the erotic.

We must postpone our own answer for a bit, since ancient Eros also took on other forms.

Pedagogy

We suddenly find Eros the son of other parents, as pederast and as founder of a way of salvation and training youth.

It is approximately 400 B.C. We are again at the Symposium of the well-bred, intellectual lords, who are making observations about love. Aristophanes has just related his tale of lovers as double beings who were cut in half, thereby becoming symbols to one another. But he is not taken seriously.

After all the observations are made, there remains one more myth about Eros. Oddly enough, in this band, it is told by a *woman,* the mysterious priestess, Diotima, who has saved Athens from the plague. She has earned the right to speak, so she relates a myth. But she does not take part in the observations.

Miss Poverty Gets the Best of Mister Cleverness

When Aphrodite (there she is again, the Greek Venus) was born, the gods held a feast, at which Poros was present: Mister Cleverness, the shrewd one, the sly fox, who always seems to find a way. That is why Kristeva also calls him "the pathfinder."

When the gods had eaten and drunk, Penia stood begging at the door. She is Miss Poverty; she has no appeal, and is turned away by the gods.

Poros is drunk and lays down by Zeus in the garden. Penia sees her chance and lays down by him and gets the best of him, going so far with him that she conceives Eros. So she must have retained at least that much appeal.

Thus Eros became a follower of beauty, because he was conceived at Aphrodite's birthday party. Because of his mother Penia, he is always poor, and far from tender and beautiful. Because of his father Poros, he is cunning, and always finds a way.

That is the new Eros myth. A shrewd, indefatigable finder of ways conceived by Miss Poverty.

Plato leaves the myth itself behind but takes up the theme in his philosophical observations. For some unknown reason or other he was to the point of philosophizing about Eros.

Members of his circles were pederasts, practitioners of "boy love." It was something between older men and young boys. Women were not included. The older Greek men had to make the young men worldly wise, they thought. The flipside was that it did not always proceed without violence, excesses, and perversions. That was also openly shared with the young men: "The old lover loves you like a wolf loves a lamb."[1] Plato calls desire — that which one feels for the enjoyment of the body of a young man — "eros" and interprets it as a sublime longing for the Higher, for the gods, for ideals such as Beauty, Truth, and the Good. In this way he directs Eros upward and removes violence, excess, and perversity from him. The erotic is henceforth a noble striving with Plato.

The others — the young men, in this case — are not loved for themselves, but as a means of rising up to eternity and immortality. Lovers are no more and no less to each other than the rungs of a ladder to heaven. A means to an end. If it is not directed upward, this eros always runs the risk of becoming violent, excessive, and perverse again, leaving the lover and the beloved behind in the poverty of Penia. But those who, through a well-directed eros, allow themselves to rise up "like the bird Pterotos" to the rarified realm of the ideal can approach true wisdom. That is Plato's way of salvation.

The pederasty of the well-bred, intellectual Greeks could also now be used as *a way of training youth:* young lovers could in this way be led on high. The noble Socrates was himself a good example.

Cut in Two Again

Four hundred years later these ideas, mixed with those of other philosophers, formed part of the Hellenistic culture in the lands around the Mediterranean Sea.

Eros was now, in *civilized circles,* the striving for the Higher. Sensual love had become the bottom rung of the ladder that leads to it. Thus lovers ascended quickly, to spiritual, more sublime forms. Higher up on the ladder one perceives how one must deal with the lower forms of love. (At best that would be something like the "art of loving," an amusing, gentlemanly pastime with women, as recommended by Ovid in his *Ars amatoria* in the first century B.C. Not something one thinks about too much; just the tricks of the upper classes for picking up lovers.) The *humane, higher, spiritual, masculine* would have a good, steadying in-

---

1. Cited by Julia Kristeva in *Histoires D'Amour* [Tales of love], with an excellent commentary (Grenoble, 1989), p. 18.

fluence on the *animal, lower, bodily, feminine.* The greater the spirit, the smaller the beast.

That ascent was not for just anyone. Certainly not for *slaves.* It is important to note that, because it is often forgotten that Hellenistic society was based on slavery. Rights were for the free. For the slaves there were no rights, no way of salvation, and no training of the youth. They were left to their lot in life. Officially, women were just as infrequently mentioned in this connection, with but a few neglected exceptions. Women know no eros and therefore also have no soul that can ascend like a bird. (Followers of Freud would say, What bird? It just means that they don't have a penis that can ascend. In a masculine society that is the only thing that counts.)

Women still have the task of being like Venus: enticing playthings, fertile, shallow, and submissive.

The Tradition of Diotima

Was that really true? I'm not so sure. The image just sketched is much too broad.

It is known that the Roman matron — within her domain, to be sure, but still — behaved in a way that was anything but submissive.

On the cultural surface, women were indeed ignored, certainly by abusive men, but there must have been exceptions. Women must have related them to each other.

It must also have been the case that there were common men with a heart. There were undoubtedly many of them who were in fact madly in love with their wives — who must have adored them. Devoted, committed couples, through thick and thin, experience, turning, mutuality. After all, life has always been stronger than any teaching.

Besides, there was that story of the birth of Eros, told by Diotima, a woman with authority. When the Athenians were suffering from the plague, she saved them.

"Just let those old philosophers blow their hot air," the common people must have thought. "We know the story that the priestess told."

70

Penia, Miss Poverty, ignored by the gods, was just too clever for the sly Poros in the end. She really got the best of him, and she got what she wanted,[2] the object of her desire, her Eros. (Too bad he went out of style.)

If those old philosophers had been open to what she had to say, Athens may have been saved from another plague. But that did not happen. They left her myth behind and ran off in their own direction.

Like the slaves, women officially had no rights according to the Hellenistic way of thinking, no way of salvation, and no pedagogy. It was, in fact, impossible. The Hellenistic way of thinking was completely dualistic; it divided reality into the good part and the bad part.

The earthly, bodily, natural, and innocent were inferior to the divine, spiritual, cultural, and technical. The bodily women belonged to the one reality, and the spiritual men to the other.

The reality of women and of common men could be nothing other than inferior, since they had only the mythical, outdated Eros of Diotima. The reality of the spiritual white men was superior, since they knew the philosophical eros of Plato, which makes the (masculine) soul — like a bird(!) — ascend sublimely on high to the gods.

Papageno

Wolfgang Amadeus Mozart's opera *The Magic Flute* (1791) is still very apropos to this way of thinking.

The realm of the night is ruled by an untrustworthy woman, the realm of the shining sun by a great, wise man. Women need male direction, if they want to get anywhere. The only nonwhite present appears to be a cunning rascal. The common Papageno is an endearing primitive bird catcher (!) who would rather not

---

2. The Dutch original plays here on the word *zin*, which means "sense," as in "the senses," "to make sense," and "sensual," but it also means "desire." Thus to get one's *zin* means "to get what one wants." *Trans.*

trouble himself with the higher things of the old philosophers. Be obedient, hold your tongue, and have lots of children.

The music is beautiful, but the story is sexist, racist, and elitist.

Dualism has been taken for granted for so long that practically no one has made the effort to investigate whether it indeed corresponds with the experiences of daily life.

Shame

The church was in a position to put an end to dualism, but it didn't happen. What a shame!

The elimination of violent temple prostitution was the obvious thing to do. But they jumped out of the frying pan and into the fire. The stream of the gospel did not find its own course, but ran into already existing dualistic beds of Hellenism. The banks of the canals and channels were expanded a bit. The course was altered somewhat here and there. But that was it. The fundamental structure of "Christianity" was Hellenistic.

But the gospel — by God! — is meant precisely for women, slaves, and common people, who can rightly place their confidence in it. The "fathers" of the church, however, were Hellenistic scholars who wanted to bring the gospel in line with their classical heritage. The "mothers" of the church were not consulted, and common fishermen had nothing more to say.

As a result, for the time being, the common people received neither right nor training for the youth. They did receive a way of salvation, but it was directed primarily to their souls and toward heaven. It would be centuries before the fire of the gospel burned through the crust of dualism.

Sensual love continued to be relegated to the lower, and therefore sinful, feminine, natural domain. It had to be lifted as quickly as possible to the higher, sublime, spiritual, masculine domain.

The depths of misery that this has caused will not be plumbed here. It is still a long way from being over. In large parts of Christendom (as well as outside of it) there is still refusal to grant rights and training to those on the lower rungs, and there is still hesitation to permit women to hold office. Sensual love continues to have a shadow of shamefulness about it. Praying is still considered a higher pursuit than making love.

And so we have reached a dead end. The first Eros leads to the temple of Venus. Common people have nothing to seek there. The next Eros, that of Diotima, is out of style, but perhaps he will come back in. The third, the Eros of the philosophers, leads finally to the rarified air of the Mountain of the Sublime, where the chapel stands with the statue of the Sublime Virgin. Perhaps there is some kind of experience to be had there, but the place is absolutely unsuitable for sensual love. Venus and the Sublime Virgin are schizoid delusions.

There is a utopian theory that claims that common, everyday love is played out somewhere between these two extremes. According to this way of thinking, a woman is always a mixture of a whore and a saint. Men are mixtures of whoremongers and devoted worshipers.

The *ars amatoria* of loving consist, then, of groping around for the golden mean. Aristotle stands here nodding approvingly. Jung wants to integrate light and shadow. Freud unleashes his neurotic theories on this problem. He has, in spite of his Jewish background, fallen under the spell of late Romantic, biological Platonism. In this he has done a great service to psychiatry, but in everyday love we run stuck with him. When we consider love a neurosis, we have missed an essential experience, or have made a fundamental error of logic.

We are helped even less if we simply turn dualism on its head, as so many countercultures have attempted to do. The sexual revolution of the sixties, for example, offered no better solution than to turn Hellenistic Eros upside down. But they let the other Eros, son of Mars and Venus, come out of his hole again. That was not their purpose, to be sure. No one is to blame. Their intentions were good. But it happened anyway, because thinking is never awarded a very high place in a counterculture. The temples of Venus were restored to honor, as a result, and not just in the form of eros centers.

Sovereign Sphere

Erotica is, by my definition, *the love that comes to expression in the enjoyment of another's body.* That is to say making love, but in a much broader sense.

73

Sexual intercourse is part of it. But so is a caress of the hair, eyes that seek each other out, a squeeze of the hand. This and so much more is no less essential.

Erotica must not be confused with sex drive. That is part of it, at the vegetative-needs level of consciousness, which displays great differences from person to person. But since I define erotica as a form of love, all the above-named essential conditions also must be present. The question is whether that is possible.

In my opinion, erotica belongs in a sovereign sphere of self-consciousness, which I would call that of "the senses." It is that broad terrain of desiring, finding pleasure in, setting one's heart on, pleasing.[3] To this realm belong the "senses"; *the only means of contact with the reality* to which we also belong.

This sphere is called sovereign because it may not be viewed as a colony of another sphere. It is not inferior (nor superior) to the two other spheres of self-consciousness: the ego and the heart. It can be called the outermost, the hedonistic perimeter of our person.

It affects not just the outside, however. If things are not in order with our senses, we become stubborn, irrational, crazy, insane, imbecilic — we are out of our senses.

So praying is not higher than making love. Those who do the one and neglect the other — where it is not a matter of necessity — are incomplete, not higher or lower. The senses have their own value and their own rights. Those who tamper with sense harm the entire person. Enticing is not inferior or dirty.

If It Is Good, It Cannot Be Good for You

And yet this idea sits very deeply with us. That is why every once in a while we will see an ad on television that comes at us from that angle, "So enticing, and yet so good for you!"

Yes, that is indeed wonderful. Enticing all by itself is suspect. After all, if it feels good, it cannot be good for you.

---

3. Again, the Dutch original uses a form of the word *zin* in each of these expressions, creating a wordplay that cannot be expressed in English. — *Trans.*

What Moves us to Love?

Earlier we pointed to the sphere of the senses as one of the filters that protects the vulnerable heart. Erotica — since it also has a place in that sphere — also has this function. It is discriminating; so many senses, so many hearts. No one loves just anyone.

But first we must examine another function of the erotic. It *moves us*.

Here a misunderstanding threatens. If the erotic has two functions, one might think that it is a means to some other end — to a higher form of love, for example. That is, in my opinion, an incorrect and objectionable thought. I maintain the sovereign character of the sphere of self-consciousness of the senses, and in so doing also that of the erotic. "Sovereign" does not, however, mean that we are talking about an inaccessible island. The erotic belongs to the whole of true love, but (once again) possesses its own independent rights. That attempts are made, albeit not necessarily, to decouple it from the whole is another problem.

Love is made possible and necessary by being-other, as we saw above. Reality is suited to love and, in fact, is propitious for it. But why would a person take a chance on love, when we know that there is always a chance that we will end up in that dangerous, obscure realm?

What moves a person to begin, to continue, to begin again where possible?

The Seven-Year Battle

I have a profound and a simple answer to this question. Because of the nature of things, a book like this ought, perhaps, to give the profound answer. But the simple should not be ignored.

It derives from folk wisdom and goes something like this: "Because she's so exquisite, because she's so exquisite, seven years I battled her love to elicit. And as long as the spoon is still in the pot, we do not despair . . ." etc. Or perhaps other words of similar gist. Seven years. That says it all.

Once more, what moves a person to love? Is it because he cannot get over his experience of reality? But reality also has some terrible cracks

75

in it and God sometimes seems to be hidden. What is it that still moves us to come out of the shadows and make ourselves vulnerable?

The friends of Plato brought, in addition to the spiritual bird Pterotos, another mythical creature to the fore: the *wolf,* the animal that suckled Romulus and Remus and swallowed Little Red Ridinghood's grandmother.

What motivates a wolf? Why does he come out of his cave?[4] Not because he loves the lamb, as the ancient pederast opined. The wolf comes out of his cave in order to satisfy his vegetative needs: hunger, thirst, sex. He has to come out, by virtue of necessity.

"Too bad," say wolfmen like Sartre and Bataille, "because whoever comes out of his cave runs into the other, who threatens him and tries to rob him of his freedom. We are condemned to each other by our vegetative needs, and especially the sex drive."

But that is, *in my opinion,* subhuman. We should not be wolves to each other, and we should make sure that we don't have to be either. *Eros desires something for his senses.* He may be beautiful, but he may not be left to himself, because then he becomes a wolf. But things do not have to be that way.

Thomas Hobbes (1625), who like Plautus before him averred the opposite and is therefore often quoted,[5] was an experience-poor British empiricist, who did not know what love was. So do not listen to him.

A person *can* be moved differently than a wolf. At least if he has been nurtured by a mother and not suckled by wolves. He need not, then, be driven perforce to reality, painfully aware of his vegetative needs. Self-consciously he *can* arrive at *more* than desires and the satisfaction of needs.

Then the other *can* be exciting. Then the other *can* be pleasing. Then she *can* not only desire, but also long and yearn that her senses be caressed. Then she will want to come out of her cave and expose herself, figuratively and literally.

Through the erotic, moreover, it *can* be possible that the more remote regions of the ego and the heart be moved. They then cast their light back on the realm of the senses, making everything even more wonderful.

4. Why does a wolf come out of his cave? He apparently never went in, but rather "wanders the thick forests and the open terrain under cover." I don't care to argue with the biologists. But my mythical wolf lives in a cave. I know that from Rudyard Kipling.

5. *Homo homini lupus* — Man is wolf to man.

The total self is now engaged. All systems go and full speed ahead. All of that *can* happen.

Seven times "can." The erotic also apparently has its own essential characteristics.

Vegetative Pressures

First, the truly erotic must have *no vegetative pressures.* The realm of the senses in the self-consciousness is always founded on the realm of the vegetative needs in the consciousness. If those needs are not met, it becomes almost impossible for the common person not to behave like a wolf.

That is easy to see where hunger is concerned. At a meal we can participate in experiences that go beyond the enjoyment of eating and drinking. If those who take part in such an event have their way, it is possible that they experience something of fellowship — even with the gods. That is why nearly all religions have ritual meals (we will return to this in Chapter 9).

None of this is achievable, however, if one or more of those participating in the meal are nearly overcome with hunger and thirst. The pressure of their vegetative needs is so great that they never get past the satisfaction of those needs.

"Eat! Drink!" is the only thing they are conscious of. They gorge themselves like wolves and do not even taste what they ingest, let alone enjoy it. The others are only an intrusion and the gods are far beyond their horizons. Until the pressure is relieved, they are in the grip of the unrelenting vegetative laws.

"Erst das Fressen, und dann die moral." First food, and then morals, Brecht said. And he was right. To a certain point.

Cruelty to Animals

The erotic — as we have defined it — can become impossible under vegetative pressure. It occurs to me that too little account has been taken of this within the relationships of lovers. "He/she wants to do it again" is sometimes complained by one lover, as though the other wants to turn on the television again to watch some boring program. But a person is not made in that way. The vegetative system cannot simply be turned on and off with the flip of a switch.

This type of hunger also causes pressure and makes it impossible to desire *more* than the satisfaction of needs. Instead of mutual pleasure, a one-sided, wolfish explosion takes place. At first that might seem exciting and exhilarating, but it must not become a unilateral custom. Then women become frigid and men become impotent.

"But if I don't want to, or can't, I surely don't have to let myself be used by someone who can't control himself." Of course not! But to leave your lover sitting under the pressure of the sexual drive is *cruelty to animals*. True love wants the other to feel pleasure; it is also *creative*.

It is very normal that lovers fall out of step with each other through sickness, accident, or biological changes, and have trouble getting in step again. But they should tell each other that and try to find a solution — with or without the help of a professional.

Unexpected Pressure

Yet how terribly difficult that can sometimes be.

When I was busy with comfort and grief,[6] I met several times with the following sad situation.

Unbearable suffering can cause very unexpected bodily reactions. In one case I was acquainted with, the suffering was the sudden death of a child, and in a couple of others the death of a partner. Normally, in situations like these, all vegetative needs are weakened and there is a complete absence of pressure.

And sometimes the opposite occurs — sexually too. That can have dramatic consequences. There were women I knew of who, in utter contrast with their habits, wanted to make love for hours on end, wild and insatiable, while their husbands were not only impotent from misery but also very upset and baffled. The poor men were going crazy: "How can you think of such a thing at a time like this? Doesn't it affect you in any way?" The reverse, in which the men's sexual needs exploded, also occurred.

6. See my *Over troosten en verdriet* [On comfort and grief] (Kampen, 1991).

78

In the general chaos and all the details of a burial there is also little time to sit and think about such things and to talk to someone about them. Hardly anyone knows that such things can happen, and almost everyone thinks it is strange, unseemly.

We have arrived at the point, it seems to me, that masturbation and the use of aids no longer present a moral problem. Neither the former nor the latter need be *a lonely adventure* if one is accompanied by a beloved. If that is not the case, no one should be surprised if the animal experiencing the cruelty attempts to relieve the pressure with someone else.

Depth

Relieving pressure is necessary, but it is not enough to caress the senses and to move the ego and the heart. There must also be *depth*. That word points to deep passages.

We met just that, for example, in Anne, who complained that she never experienced anything with Thomas, "not even during sex." Thomas never achieved the level of experience. As far as he was concerned they had also probably only eaten food together, they never really had a meal. Bread was bread. Wine was wine. Never anything else. I eat, you eat, he eats, we eat. Bon appetit.

When we elaborated the idea of the left and right hand of the self-consciousness, we spoke a little about the two ways in which the senses worked: the technical and the open. The first is precise and discriminating, and is a condition for effective action. The second enters the *depths* and makes experience possible in the sovereign sphere of the senses. And there, in the depths, we also find the deep passages, the connecting corridors between the ego and the heart.

Whether those spheres are in fact reachable depends on other essential conditions than those established for the erotic. We will come back to that in Chapters 7 and 8.

All the Senses, Every Sense

There are many women who complain that their lover is apparently equipped with only one erotic organ, his penis. Normally women want to delve the erotic depths of love *with all their senses and with their whole body.* Some men seem never to want anything more than a quick ejaculation — straight up, straight down. "Wonderful, honey. Good night, and spare me all that crap about foreplay and afterplay" (Levi Weemoedt).

If this is not a lack of depth, it certainly is an odd way to behave, and comes very close to the conduct of a wolf.

If such a man is so dense that he simply does not know how to delve the depths, a woman can still try to teach him. Then she will know right away whether or not he actually belongs to her erotic type.

The last essential condition to be named is very closely related to this: the erotic cannot be separated from the rest of the sensual sphere of self-consciousness. It will always be part of it. An erotic relationship that does not touch on the other aspects of the sensual sphere is impossible. It rends the sensual sphere into rags and reduces the other to one or another of his or her essential parts. *The erotic is inseparable from the rest of the sensual sphere.* We will return to this in Chapter 10.

One for Each of the Senses

An almost unbelievable example is Peter, who has a different woman for each one of the senses.

Olive is a faithful wife through thick and thin. She is a first-rate cook, keeps an orderly house, and makes sure that he looks his best each day.

In addition to this housewife, he has a good-looking babe. He lets himself be seen with her every once in a while, but he almost never touches her (so he says).

He also has a woman "to make passionate love to." And (why, but of course!) he has a female pen pal, with whom he corresponds about deep subjects; as well as a culture woman, with whom he shares a season pass to the local theater; a hiking woman, with whom he enjoys backpacking, complete with light-weight camping gear. (I'm surprised that he does not have a traveling woman, or a church woman. But Peter too has his limits.)

Since he is a nice, interesting, and striking man — a man with a real *joie de vivre* — all the ladies find him attractive. Except Olive, that is. But she is known as a jealous old prude in his circles. That is why she came to me to complain. But what can I say? Dependent as she is, she dares not rebel. She just wants to know that she is right.

I can put her mind at rest: "He is a fragmented man. That is why he is incapable of taking the risk of true, complete love and dares not permit himself more than a bunch of loose contacts. Whoever seeks to do something with many does it all with none. What he and his "lovemaking woman" have together is, *as far as I am concerned,* not worthy of the name *erotica.*"

"It isn't? What do you call it then?"

"Sex. I will explain it more later."

Erotic Characteristics

Everyone has his or her own erotic characteristics. That is why some find us very attractive and others find us disgusting, and others tolerate us in the vein of "sure, he's OK." And here again it is the case that hunger makes raw bones taste good.

The erotic is *selective,* for itself, for the ego, and for the heart. And it must be allowed to be such, otherwise we have problems with clogs.

Appearance

A body cannot bear every glance. We sometimes shiver when we are looked at, especially if we are naked. Nor can every eye look with love and longing at every body.

Our glance is almost reflexively drawn to what we find attractive and turns away from that which appears unattractive. Both are very personally determined, but there are also subculturally determined erotic models. We must look like them if we want to be enticing and desirable.

81

It gives a slight advantage on the street to those who measure up. Whole industries owe their existence to them.

It also gives a slight disadvantage in love to the handicapped, who do not measure up. *They must find love with those who know how to look deeply.*

Because true love is not blind. On the contrary. Those who naively say so have not understood love. True love gives us the ability to look through appearances to behold the true nature of the beloved. But normally, on the street, people do not look deeply.

In spite of the existence of popular, erotic models, tastes differ enormously. One likes them fat, another likes them thin. A certain movement, which provokes a reflexive shiver of pleasure in one, provokes irritation in another. (Under)clothes that create excitement in one create endless distaste in another. Lovers know what their partners like. They must keep it in mind, not only to set love in motion but especially to keep it in motion.

But is the beloved not the most desirable in the world? To be sure, to be sure. That is the result of looking deeply and arriving at — through the deep passages — the ego and the heart. But that is not to say that lovers must not do their best to remain desirable for each other.

"My mother does not use makeup anymore, and she does not go to the hair salon as frequently as she used to. After all, she already has her security," said a young girl whose mother was living with a man. Then in the long run things will certainly not go well.

I also include the *voice* with the erotic characteristics that make up appearance. Here too there is no arguing with taste. Some voices sound like the voices of angels to us, while others sound like squawking crows. Between the two there is a whole spectrum of variations. Not all ears are equally discriminating, nor is everyone prepared to listen deeply.

Temperament

Appearance is, however, just one of several erotic characteristics, and not even the most important, I think. Those who find themselves unattractive at first sight and hearing and have no lover may not agree. But they still always have the chance of meeting someone who does not reject them at first sight and hearing.

The *temperament,* as an erotic characteristic, offers far fewer chances.

You cannot look beyond the temperament. It either fits or it does not. The term is used in this book in two senses.

The older understanding of temperament was "the correct mixture of the four bodily fluids" or humors: blood (sange), yellow gall (chole), black gall (melanchole) and phlegm (flegma). The dominant fluid supposedly determined the character of the person: sanguine, choleric, melancholic, and phlegmatic. That theory has been abandoned. In this book, temperament, as an erotic characteristic, is primarily *the whole of inborn possibilities that determine parameters of the character*.

This can be further refined by love and the sharp edges can be taken off. (In a bad relationship the sharp edges are filed to a razor's edge.) But the temperament itself cannot be pried apart.

I am who I am

Once inside a loving relationship, one must be very careful with appealing to temperament.

"You have to accept me just as I am. That is just who I am. I am who I am." In love, those are dangerous statements. They make a person untouchable. "I am who I am!" It sounds like God talking! At least he spoke from complete accessibility.

We are not what we could be. The temperament is a given, but the character we form from it is our own responsibility. In love, we can and must continue to shape and polish it.

Here too tastes differ. What one defines as tranquil, another rejects as listless. What one finds wonderfully exciting, the other calls weird and kinky. The same is true for sensitive and wimpy. And so on.

The temperament is like the face. The distinguishing lines do not change over the years, but become more pronounced and expressive. Many people have not paid attention to this fact, and have not been selective enough where the erotic is concerned. "Things will work out with time. Love conquers all," they thought. But they were wrong.

For the second sense of the term "temperament," I will make use of a variation on the classic description. Temperament as an erotic characteristic can be understood as *the unique nature and composition of the bodily fluids that play a role in the erotic,* such as saliva, perspiration, vaginal fluid, sperm, and other derivatives. Their taste and smell are very specific and bring ecstasy to one and revulsion to another, with all imaginable reactions in between.

The human organs of smell and taste stand in direct relation to the seat of the emotions in the central nervous system and play a very large role in the erotic. After all, the secret art of manufacturing love-inducing perfumes is older than philosophy! The perfume industry has misled many a beginner in the ways of love to confuse the scents of Opium and Chanel with those of the temperament.

Skin

The last and best example of an erotic characteristic is the skin.

Lovemaking consists, after all, in the rubbing of erotically sensitive (erogenous) skin against skin. But here again, not all skin bears all skin, let alone finds its attractive.

Moreover, needs are very different. One wants frequent and intimate touching, hugging, stroking, fondling, and kissing; the other could take it or leave it.

It is here a matter of individual erotic characteristics that are partially shaped by upbringing and the subculture in which one grows up.

There are families where there is never any hugging and kissing, not even with the children. Mother is rather cold and distant, and if father feels the need, he meets it behind closed doors.

I even know of a number of average families that seldom or never touch each other. Relatives and family members will sometimes shake hands and on very important occasions a quick kiss. That is their code of conduct. But those who grow up in such families develop a definite do-not-touch disposition. Of course, the opposite can also occur.

A very remarkable development is that after the overwhelming number of incest scandals in the late 1980s, a number of frightened fathers suddenly began keeping their daughters of six years and older at a certain distance, "because before you know it, they are accusing you of incest."

Skin as Barrier

There are those who have "oceanic" experiences of love, as an attempt at dissolution and unification with the beloved person or thing. They seek to cause themselves to disappear in a greater, more comprehensive whole, and finally, in the mother ocean, the All.

They experience their skin, the wonderful, attractive skin of the lover, as a final hurdle that prevents them from achieving complete oneness. The skin is the barrier that *separates* the lovers, they think. In the sensation of skin on skin, they are right next to each other, and yet so far away from each other.

Only once! Only once during reproduction was oneness achieved, when the little spermatozoa, "das Tierchen so hübsch und froh," dissolved itself in the egg, in the waters of the mother ocean, to become one. Sadly, sadly, immediately thereafter the one was doomed by the skin to powerless loneliness, damned since then by the skin to live apart.

According to oceanic lovers, a person is always longing to *re*live that one ur-moment of bliss. That is, according to them, the single motivation for love — an attempt to achieve oneness, which always fails because the skin intervenes.

These thoughts cause us to hail back to the tale of Aristophanes. He too considered love a longing for a lost paradisiacal existence, a regressive striving.

It seems to me superfluous to explain here again that these thoughts are alien to me. We do not disappear in love, but come into our own right and thus to our true selves. Love is not a vain, lonely, regressive longing, but a happiness-producing, mutual way of living. Not regressive, but prospective. The future shines on us! Pleasant places again await me.

Being other does not render love impossible, but guarantees it. The skin of the beloved is *not an erotic barrier, but the point of encounter*. There osmosis takes place: erotic, narcissistic, and shulamithic.

A Sack of Skin, Filled with Blood and Guts

The oceanic view of love is *pessimistic:* The poor lover has only the skin of the beloved. He can go no farther. The reality which he seeks is inaccessible, hidden behind it.

There is another, equally pessimistic view, that says, "*There is nothing hidden behind it.* There is just the surface. Sensual love is an illusion, you're better off getting knockdown drunk."

That was, for example, what the young monks told themselves, when they were seeing double from vegetative pressures and were nauseous with guilt, tossing and turning on their wooden planks.

"Just think about it," they would tell themselves, "use your imagination. What is it that you actually desire? A rotting sack of skin, and that's all. And what is in that sack? A stinking mess. You get sick just thinking about it. Slime, blood, guts, bones. Ugh! Just let your soul ascend to the sublime."

Now everybody is back on stage. The Hellenists with their dualism have again made their appearance.

Osmosis

Our vision is optimistic. The skin is the erotic point of encounter *par excellence*. That is why lovers are willing to expose themselves. Naked skin longs to touch naked skin — the whole body is erogenous.

The wolf is incapable of this. Only at the height of his sexual drive does he flop out a small piece of naked skin in order to stick it in another small piece of naked skin accessible only for this purpose. But with people it *can* be very different.

By means of the skin *osmosis* can occur. The warmth of the blood is shared. Blood that is *nephesh,* that is soul. They breathe each other's breath; *ruach,* spirit. The feel each other's heartbeat; *leb,* resolve. The bodily fluids, the *humor,* of the lovers are osmotically mixed through the skin. That is the moment that Klimt tried to capture.

"Omne animal post coitum triste," Aristotle is supposed to have said. After intercourse, all animals are sad. And he added: "praeter gallum, qui cantat," except the rooster, who crows.

But if after making love *both* lovers are not happy, satisfied, and contented, they have not achieved their full potential.

Another industry has developed around the question, How can I have that generally erotically desirable skin? A question that seems at least as important to me is, How do I find someone who thinks it wonderful to touch me, who makes my fingers tingle when I touch his skin and with whom I can find depth?

The Erotic Type

A person's erotic characteristics make them a certain *erotic type*. That is not coterminous with the place where one must seek someone to love — *that circle is much smaller* — but is the type that one finds attractive, appealing. Before one loves, it is necessary first to make sure that there is a match where this is concerned. Especially those who are somewhat older and have a few disappointments behind them must be fully aware of this.

When they (finally) find someone who confirms their ego, they immediately think it very special. Under the influence of the vegetative pressures and because they are so terribly happy and excited finally to have found someone that opens to them a wider perspective, they rush to the conclusion that slight erotic dislike or uneasiness will soon be put in order. "I just have to get over it, I'll get used to it. It will work out." It is not only homophiles who think that way. Perhaps in the last few years they the least of all.

To have to overcome something erotically is life threatening. In a limited sense, however, it is not uncommon that lovers need some time to experiment with each other erotically before they get to know how to satisfy each others' needs. Yet it should not take too long. I would think a matter of days. If erotic distaste continues beyond that point, it will not eventually go away but become stronger.

The person who does violence to himself in this way will eventually do violence to the other as well — albeit sometimes very subtly. Moreover, true osmotic *reconciliation* after a falling out becomes almost impossible.

Erotic Fascination

Another trap is that of *erotic fascination*. The mutual recognition of erotically compatible people occurs almost instinctively. Those who are self-conscious in this regard can relax and go about things with complete freedom. But those who are not, or who are not able, can easily imagine themselves in love and jump in over their heads in some wild goose chase. That is especially true during periods of personal difficulty or problems in a marriage.

Those who passively surrender themselves to their reflexes are on the same behavioral level as the wolf after a bitch in heat. It can be very persuasive under the influence of vegetative pressure, alcohol, or naiveté, but it is well below the human level.

Sex

Repeatedly I have stated in this book that, *in my opinion,* one can only speak of love where the heart is engaged and applied. That is the first and most important essential condition.

Then I have argued that the erotic is a form of love. But can the first essential characteristic be maintained? Is that not too harsh in the light of the many today who simply want to enjoy each others' bodies without going on to love, without drawing up some kind of we-covenant?

It is, of course, also a question of semantics, but not just that. We lapse into a hopeless confusion of tongues if we begin to call *detached erotica* a form of love. I prefer to reserve the term *sex* for that.

Do I have something against sex? That depends. There are all kinds and all shapes of sex; for sale and for free; from the kind, tender and mutual, to the wolfish — perverse, violent, and excessive.

But this book is not at all about sex. This book is about love, and for the sensual form of love, I reserve the term *erotic.* I could have turned the terms around. I could have used other terms, just as long as *the same word is not used to describe these two very different forms of human interaction.* They are not homonyms, and that is perhaps what separates me from the young man in the white jacket. He says "love" and means "sex."

But let's slow down. I am getting ahead of myself.

Erotic Investment

Much of what seems to fall outside of the essential conditions can actually be placed under the rubric of the erotic, and therefore of love — for example, the erotic investment.

In order to know whether two people actually belong together, some kind of beginning must be made, because, as the English say, "the proof of the pudding is in the eating."

If there is hope of love, but no certainty that there is love, or that it will come, an investment must be made in the ego and the heart of the other. Investments are always risky, but nothing ventured, nothing gained.

Many girls and women have been devastated when they discovered they were pregnant and the investment was not returned. They found either that they were completely incompatible or that the man had managed to get the girl in bed with flattery, without having made any investment himself. For the one it was erotic, but for the other it was just plain sex.

In the past it was thought that they should marry, and often they thought so too. And the women continued investing. Sometimes the investment was paid back with interest. That happened too, but not very often.

Heartbreaking.

These asymmetrical relationships — erotic investment for one, sex for the other — still appear, but at least no one is obliged to continue them anymore. The old Calvinistic "right to revolt" is increasingly recognized in such cases. I think that is gain.

Some people are quick to trust, take on risks easily, and therefore very easily and quickly make an erotic investment. Others are vulnerable and therefore more cautious. They first want some kind of security deposit. That is a difference in temperament and does not diminish the value of this form of erotica.

Erotic Play

There are two friends who do not love each other. They are aware of that and have no illusions. But they do enjoy sex and for that reason are drawn to each other.

And yet that is too narrow for them. What they really want is erotica, with the ego and the heart and all that it entails. Then they *play* that they are in love, like children play that they are father and mother, and the cat is the baby. They leave behind their day-to-day world for what it is and together enter another world. But someday they will have to come out again, and that is frequently very difficult on the morning after, "the morning after the night before."

89

Sometimes illusions begin to creep in with one or the other. Sometimes the change from the play world to the everyday world is too abrupt. Then they keep on playing, with the help of a string of partners, who do not even really have to exist.

A play world very easily crosses over into fantasy world. Then it makes no difference with whom one makes love. It is always a fantasy lover. And only the fantasy lover brings climax.

The boundaries between the play world and the fantasy world are not always clearly marked. What happens there is — *in my opinion* — erotica. Not sex.

The mythical Narcissus, with whom we will deal in the following chapter, knows more about this, and about the world of imagination.

7. Narcissus

Like a Flower

Suddenly, Narcissus has appeared within the horizons of the European world of experience. An odd chap from Greek Boeotia — with whom everyone must attempt to come to terms in love.

He is honored and maligned — but mostly maligned. His tale is often repeated. The German psychiatrists of the nineteenth century linked his name to a stage of development and to a problem of development: narcissism.

Around 1980, the authoritative Christopher Lasch even attempted to analyze the crisis of Western culture as a result of the spell under which this mysterious, handsome young man has placed us.[1] Julia Kristeva sees him blossoming in the gardens of Bernard of Clairvaux and Thomas Aquinas and also in Spinoza's flowerpot.[2]

Narcissus has arisen from the dead *like a flower* (there are 20,000 known varieties of narcissus, which grow in all types of soil; all varieties need ample water). But first a broad outline of the myth. It was told at the beginning of the Christian era by Ovid. He suspected already then that he would soon be exiled, or worse. Perhaps that thought may have influenced the course of this tale.

1. See Christopher Lasch, *The Culture of Narcissism: American Life in an Age of Diminishing Expectations* (New York: Norton, 1978).

2. See Julia Kristeva, *Tales of Love,* trans. Leon S. Roudiez (New York: Columbia University Press, 1987).

Echo

The mother of Narcissus is the lily-like nymph Liriope, and his father the river god Cesiphus. Water would continue to play an important role in his life.

There is also another nymph in his life: Echo. She is pretty enough, but there is something about her. She has been punished for her big mouth and now she can only repeat the last word of what others say. And so those who talk to her only hear themselves. Some think it is ideal, because you can make her say what you want to hear.

But *Narcissus does not want that.* It is important to establish that first. He wants no monologue. It does not suit him. Later he will be told that he can only love himself, but that does not seem right to me. Still, he is accused of spurning Echo. Is it perhaps because he is not prepared to listen to himself? That *double entendre* never quite disappears from this myth.

Scorned

Things are not going well for Echo. "Scorned, she hides in the forest, ashamed, she hides her face among the branches and then conceals herself in quiet caverns. Her passion remains, indeed, grows due to the pain of being scorned. Nights of sleepless worry leave her body emaciated, want wrinkles her skin, her life fluids are drained from her body. Only voice and bones remain — and then only voice. The bones, they say, became stone. . . . She can be heard by all, it is only sound that lives on in her."[3]

"Oh, my dear people," I think to myself when I read this sad story, "oh, Rita and the many others. Be sure that you have something of your own to say, or else you will be condemned to be a lonely echo of everyone else, especially of false therapists."

3. Ovid, *Metamorphoses*, trans. Rolfe Humphries (Bloomington: Indiana University Press, 1955).

"Is there no other for me?" Echo must have thought, but she could not move the words over her lips. No, there was no other, no woman and no man.

Narcissus Meets His Ego

What is wrong with Narcissus then? Nothing! He is just preoccupied with himself. A little too much, perhaps? No matter. But it will be held against him. The goddess of revenge utters the curse: "He will love himself and never possess his lover." (I rather think that more a blessing than a curse. Oh well.)

Hot and thirsty from hunting, Narcissus bends over the *mirror-like water* of a spring. What he sees there surprises and delights him. Finally he is confronted with *the image* of the one for whom he is longing. The ideal lover! At last! The hunt is finally over. He has found his destiny, indeed. Thank the gods.

But the dialogue with his lover does not go well. In a dramatic monologue he comes to the realization that what he takes for someone else is nothing other than his own image in the reflecting water. He, the desirable one, who spurned Echo as his lover, realizes not only that he cannot get away from himself in love, but also that the image of his beloved dissolves into nothing — disappears — when he moves away from the spring.

That is too much for him. What he understood as true love is impossible. He can no longer live, and strikes his breast with his strong hands, which "gleam like marble" until his heart stops.

He dies at the edge of the reflecting spring. The wails of the river nymphs, "his sisters," reach poor Echo in her quiet cave. She understands what has happened and echos their cries. There is nothing else she can do.

But when they arrive to burn Narcissus, his body is gone. He has risen from the dead, and at the place of his death a flower blooms, which is reflected in the quiet water.

Here we are again. Without noticing and against our wishes, we are again lost in that obscure part of the Land of Love. Or are we?

I'm Here Too

The sovereign sphere of self-consciousness called ego lies between that of the heart and the senses. It has its own rights and its own worth. Those who take this too casually inflict injury on themselves or on love and block up the deep accesses to the heart.

The erotic is founded on (conditioned) reflexes. The love-seeking ego — "Narcissus" — yearns, weighs, ponders, chooses for or against, and takes *responsibility*. If that is not the case with someone who claims to be looking for love, then we speak of a weak ego or of deception (cross out what does not apply, and don't kid yourself!).

Eros without "depth" (Eros w.d. we will call it from now on) only wants something delectable for his senses.

Narcissus wants more. He wants someone for his ego, a "partner" fit for him and for whom he is fit. He wants mutual affinity. That can happen only if the other has access to his world of meaning and experience and he to the other's. Then the lovers no longer "possess" each other — and in this sense the curse was not a curse — but their lives become intertwined. And so they grow closer to each other, as they experience that the other is part of their ego. If they should unexpectedly lose each other — to nonlife or to death — it is as though they have lost part of themselves. That is called ego-loss,[4] and is grounds for mourning. Needless to say, a person can also become attached to things, plants, animals, ideas, expectations, and especially to a career. But we are not talking about that now.

If Narcissus lacks depth, he remains the prisoner of his senses and of his ego, the ultimate consumer. We will call him Narcissus w.d., but we'll leave him for later consideration.

Things did not go well for the Narcissus of Ovid. *Was that inevitable or did he make mistakes?*

- Can my ego love the other as is, or do I merely see myself in a *mirror?*

---

4. By "ego-loss" I mean that a person can lose a part of himself or herself, as it were; another person, an animal, a plant or a thing, an expectation, a job. Thereafter, the person must find himself or herself again through a difficult grieving process. See W. ter Horst, *Over troosten en verdriet* [On comfort and grief] (Kampen, 1991).

- Can my ego love the other as is, or am I overcome by the power of an *image* that is self-fabricated, or fabricated by another, but is inaccessible since it does not really exist?
- Can my ego love the other as is, or am I condemned to nothing other than *self-love?*

These three eternal, penetrating questions are of highest importance for those egos who are prepared to take the wager of love. My answer is that *it is possible, if. . . .* And then there come a few essential conditions, which have already in part been mentioned.

The Narcissus of Ovid made two fatal mistakes.

First, *he did not recognize himself in his reflection.* That speaks of a comprehensive lack of self-understanding. Such a person is incapable of love. Second, *he did not peer through to the bottom of the spring.* He had apparently not learned to look deeply. You probably do not learn such things when your mother is a nymph who just splashes around naked in the water, and your father is a god who is always busy with other streams.

No matter what the case, in this chapter we will try to find answers to the question regarding what we must do with the love-seeking ego, with Narcissus. How does he come into his own right? What are the essential conditions that have to be met if we want to answer the first part of the three questions affirmatively?

In other words, how can we avoid repeating this myth?

Mirror, Mirror

Mirrors, the good kind at least, are essential in life — and therefore especially in love, which is the most condensed form of life. Mirrors, however, can possess puzzling and even magical qualities. Ovid's Narcissus was neither the first nor the last to discover that fact. We know more stories about mirrors.

In certain parts of the Dutch province of Drenthe it is still the custom that a cloth is draped over the mirror if there is a death in the house. Why? To protect the relatives from their own reflection? Or is there a primal fear that the image of the dead might suddenly loom in the mirror? What has such a mirror absorbed over the course of the years, and what might it be hiding?

Ancient mirrors, like their human counterparts, have their own characteristics. They were polished pieces of some metal or another, not completely even, with dull spots. Earlier, people looked at such mirrors with intrigue. What might it be a reflection of? Was it real? "But then we shall see face to face," Paul promised us.[5]

There are spooky tales about people who lose their mirror image or bargain it away. E. T. A. Hoffman[6] mentions General Suwarow and especially the ego-weak Erasmus Spikher. He had an affair with the dangerous Giulietta, to whom he lost his mirror image. And so she gained power over him. It did not go at all well with that man from then on. But we will leave that for now.

Small children love to pull funny faces in the mirror and wonder, "Can I really look like that?"

Teenagers can stand naked for hours in front of the mirror studying every line of their bodies, sometimes with satisfaction, more frequently with anxiety. "Is that me? What is happening to me?" (breasts, pubic hair, facial hair, muscles).

People who have no mirror in their houses, or who never use it, should not be trusted in love. They do not dare to look at their own ego. How can they love another ego? So those who want to avoid the same fate as Ovid's Narcissus must provide themselves with a mirror and look at it frequently. But they'd better make sure it is a good one, because some — laugh-mirrors, cry-mirrors, magic-mirrors — unbearably distort and discolor reality.

What You See Is What You Are

When children exchange insults, they often reply, "What you say is what you are!" There is ancient wisdom in this, because before it is said, it is seen. *We see in the other what is in ourselves.*

If that idea is taken to its extreme, it can get out of hand. That has repeatedly occurred, in the course of time, under the influence of (Neo)platonism and gnosticism, right up to our present time. Then the

---

5. 1 Corinthians 13:12.
6. In Eichendorff, Hoffmann, et al., *"Uit het leven van een nietsnut" en ander verhalen* ["From the life of a good-for-nothing" and other stories] (Utrecht: Prisma, n.d.), p. 98.

Other, the other, and others are reduced to sensual illusions, reflections of the autonomous ego. Then we are coming close again to our friend Vincent and the Phoenix.

But there is still much truth in it. The beloved is not only a moon that dimly reflects the sunlight of love. She also reflects the structure of the true pattern and the chaos of the cracks. In the beloved, Narcissus always meets himself. *Lovers are mirrors of one another.* That has important consequences.

First, it entails that when one fights with one's beloved, one must consult oneself. Do I perhaps recognize something of myself in that which offends me in the other? After all, those who see their own reflection and do not recognize themselves are committing the same mistake as Ovid's Narcissus.

There are, for example, people who from their youth have continually ruined promising relationships for more or less the same reason. It could be that they just happen to have bad luck each time, but statistically the chance is much greater that they constantly enter into conflict with the reflection of their own ego. This can be corrected with the help of a good psychotherapist, in individual or group session.

Love and Therapy Do Not Mix

Never let your beloved one take on the role of the therapist. That will definitely turn out badly.

Among my female students there were some who continually lapsed into this role. Hearty, healthy, happy women, who always saw a potential lover in the promising young men, whose promise never really materialized due to various psychological problems. "I can help him," they thought. Sure, they could, and the young men were also happy with that. But what did they actually see in each other?

They then made a weak stab at a mixture of love and psychotherapy. These two relationships do resemble each other, but there is also a very big essential difference. The psychotherapeutic relationship is — in contrast to love — of a temporary nature. A good therapist makes herself superfluous as quickly as possible. And that is what my students also did.

When the men, thanks to great, sometimes year-long invest-ments on the part of the women, overcame their problems, they no longer needed their therapists. They quickly fell in love with another, less hearty woman and sorrowfully said their goodbyes. "I have a lot to thank you for and I will never forget you."

Lack of gratitude? Not at all. Just a lack of self-understand-ing and insight.

"But why couldn't he love the woman in me when he over-came his problems?"

"Because a man and a woman can forgive a lot, but not the fact that one has actually grown up under the care of the other."

Selective, Distorting, and Discoloring

Not all human mirrors are the same. Not by a mile. What were the characteristics of the mirror that Narcissus looked into?

There is a very important moment of decision wrapped up with true love. *What does the ego see, when it looks in the mirror of the other?* Itself, but what of itself?

Every human mirror is selective, distorting, and discoloring. It is, after all, a mirror with a history. All kinds of things have happened to it, both good and bad. Therefore there are both dull and highly polished spots. Cracks and discoloring are also present. *Not everyone can use every mirror.*

In one mirror I am flattered and encouraged by what I see. In another I see my flaws and begin to despise myself. There are also mirrors in which I do not recognize myself at all. "Is that me? I don't want to look like that!" Now I just have to be careful not to lose my mirror image, like poor old Erasmus Spikher.

Nevertheless, if Narcissus has complete self-understanding and looks into the mirror of true love, then his ego is affirmed. That means that his true nature comes to light. The cracks are also visible, but in such a way that he gains the courage to do something with them and about them. *The mirror of the true beloved reflects an encouraging image.*

Keep an eye out, then, and do not be satisfied with anything less. And if your beloved one is not encouraged by what he or she sees, try polishing up your own mirror.

Ideal or Sterile

Ovid's Narcissus had the nearly ideal situation. It is hard to believe that he still made a mistake.

"There was a clear spring, in which the water shimmered like silver. Neither the shepherds nor the sheep that grazed on the hills, nor any cattle had yet drunk from it. The watery mirror was undisturbed by any bird or animal and no tree branch had ever fallen into it. Around it lay a grassy rim, which drew its moisture from the spring; and so the grass was always green. Moreover, the trees let no sunlight through. Here the handsome youth laid down in order to catch his breath from the hunting party and to drink from the spring."[7]

Here the perfect Neoplatonic mirror is held before us; the "speculum sin macula" that is also mentioned in the Book of Wisdom.[8] In it, we are all supposed to recognize ourselves face to face.

But apparently we do not. I suppose that is because this mirror is impersonal and therefore sterile and doomed to lovelessness.

The Power of Images

Ovid's Narcissus saw an image and was immediately struck by it — and even more than that. "That is it!" he knew. In popular parlance that is called — at least when it has a mutual character — love at first sight.

That he saw his own image in the water (the element of his parents), has nothing to do with it. *We are dealing here with the unique power of the image in love.* There are many stories of this sort known to us all. They are usually told when it actually comes to (the point of) love, but there are surprisingly many, and they all resemble each other.

7. Ovid, *Metamorphoses*.
8. Wisdom 7:26.

"That's Her!"

She steps out of a small blue car into the winter sunshine. She looks briefly behind her and says something to someone whom I cannot see. Her blue eyes shine like stars, and she laughs gently.

She is wearing a long, dark brown winter coat, and her red curls shine like gold in the sun. Then she firmly closes the car door.

"My God," I think to myself, "how is it possible? That's her!"

That is how it affected me when I first beheld the image of Els. That is why I still tell it in the present tense, the "historic present." Such a moment may never take on anything of the past. But if we do not use it sparingly, that can indeed happen.

Recognition

Immediately they were struck by the sight of each other. How is that possible?

Much thought has been devoted to this subject and even more books. One of the ideas that is most agreeable to me is that such persons actually *recognize* each other at such a moment. That can only occur because they have loved each other before.

As children they were already crazy about each other. Hand in hand they walked along the beach and through the blooming flower garden. They comforted each other when they were sad, and they listened to each other's secret desires. Sometimes they played hide-and-go-seek under the stars of the Milky Way or they swam together in the clear blue water of the mother sea. There they picked the rare sea roses and searched the elusive oyster shells for mysterious, shining pearls. They did not desire these for themselves, but they gave them to each other as pledges. They were then carefully concealed in the hidden places of their lives.

And when the erotic was awakened in them, they desired each other. Together they discovered how they must express their love, and so they found perfect love. Naturally!

And all that time they yearned for the day when they would actually meet.

"So, you do exist!"

"Yes, I exist, just for you."

Imagination and Realization

So — in one way or another — a person creates the dream image of his or her beloved. (Dream here is not the sleepy dream of Freud, but the visionary dream of the prophet Joel and of Martin Luther King Jr.)

That occurs in the creative world of *imagination,* of course. We sometimes imagine the most impossible things. All of civilization, before it became a reality, was first imagined and then realized in day-to-day life. Why could the same not occur with the dream of the beloved?

Two Dreams

It can also happen that two completely separate dream images arise. The one is of the sublime exalted sort, who can only be imagined, the other is that delectable piece, with whom only perverse, excessive, and violent things can be done.

This seems to occur mostly in people who have experienced a spartan upbringing, with a lot of emphasis on duty and little room for pleasure. But that does not explain everything. Some seem to be born with a certain tendency toward this split image.

For those people who possess two dream images, it is extremely difficult to apply them in the day-to-day reality of love, because no matter who they meet, the one is never good enough and the other never satisfies.

The suggestion that these dream images derive from some previous life or from some collective reservoir of consciousness does not attract me much as a pedagogue. I prefer to address those who nurture the child, and later the adult children, as the ones who are responsible for the resulting dream image.

That is difficult, because every (sub)culture creates its own model dream image, and you could even say imposes it. Those who want to belong must have these and no other ideas about the imagined, the dreamed, the ideal lover.

A good example of this is the Medici Venus. All the dream women of Western intellectuals began to resemble her. We do not see her much anymore, but how many other dream images did not later derive their sleepy eyes from Greta Garbo, their full lips from Brigitte Bardot, and that defiant look from Madonna? And how many of those beer-drinking boys, who during their weekends drove from bar to bar in old cars with red faces, derived from each other — let us say by peer pressure — their image of how the perfect woman ought to be? ("A whore in bed, a child at home, and a lady in public." Yes, even today!)

Such externally imposed traits hinder the free imagination. They lend to the dream image of the beloved a mummy-like quality. Zombie, they now say, under the influence of Voodoo culture. But that is not what I mean here. A zombie is the living dead, a mummy is the dead living.

In love it becomes a real obstacle, because a mummy cannot be related to day-to-day life. A mummy does not change through the different phases of life's journey. *The more the dream image bears the traits of a mummy, the more difficult it is to relate it to a living person.* A dream image that can no longer be applied to day-to-day life has become an illusion. That is true in religion, in art, and in love.

Bad Experience

It is not, however, only these externally derived, imposed traits that hinder free imagination. Bad experiences in one's love life can also leave traces in the dream image.

The fossilizing effect of a bad love experience is much more dangerous than that of the imposed model image, because with a little luck — and a lot of courage — those who want to can avoid the pressure of their environment, while those who want to free themselves from a painful past must make an enormous effort. Not everyone can or wants to do that.

Here we run up against the defensive reactions again. Not only do they act like plugs in stopping up the deep access to the heart, but they also fossilize certain features of the dream image. And in the end it amounts to the same thing.

Carte Blanche

Creeps like the incestuous father, the smothering mother, the pretty, catty sister, that tease of a brother, the sadistic, dominating friend, and the dirty pastor whose hands are never still all belong to the dark region and will remain there without further mention. But they do exist and can very well have such a mummifying effect on the dream image that every initial recognition of a lover ends in disappointment upon further examination.

"For a minute there, I thought: 'That's him, finally that's him!' But later I realized that no, that wasn't him after all."

Those loveless creeps are sometimes used as excuses, however, by those who are too weak or too lazy to get a grip on themselves when things go amiss in love. I even know of those who have created such a rotten past in order not to have to be responsible *here and now*.

When the escape route is removed through an extensive look into family history, they escape to a previous existence. Suddenly, so it seems, they were sexually abused several centuries ago. Thus they write themselves a carte blanche to behave as they please.

Positive Experiences

Positive love experiences free the imagination. What results is a living dream image that can be attained in day-to-day life. Now the appearance of the beloved can be freely recognized.

Sometimes that occurs in a moment, as we described above. Sometimes it takes longer, and one must spend a lot of time with the other in order finally to come to the discovery that "this is real."

Pedagogically we must attach a great deal of importance to the early childhood years. That is something that we dealt with earlier in another context. Every loving ego-definition is in one way or another contoured to the dream image.

The Indian with the Painted Face

That is a little known fact, I have noticed. Four young mothers and I stood looking at a large group of toddlers who were playing wonderfully with each other at an Indian party. One of the boys tripped over a protruding root of a tree, and fell smack on his nose. The hot dog that he had so patiently roasted on a stick over the open fire fell in the sand. He howled from pain and disappointment. A beautifully painted little Indian girl, more or less his age, gave him a kiss and said something that made him smile again.

"How sweet," said one of the mothers. "Too bad I don't have my camera with me, because when he gets older he won't remember any of this!"

"That is not so bad," I said. "Pictures are great for personal histories. But there is something far more essential. All such experiences share the characteristic that even when there is no more memory of them, something of them remains. And that which remains is precisely the real: the inspiring and the perspective-giving. That boy will never lose this moment. That girl will be taken up into his world of imagination and will play a part in the creation of his future dream image. His lover may well bear the traits of an Indian with a painted face."

They looked at me a bit oddly. "You haven't lost any of the love experiences that you have had. No one can take them away from you, even when you no longer remember them," I tried again.

They had never looked at it in that way.

Later I tried the idea on some of the fathers who were providing transportation for the party. They did not seem to have a clue either. What you cannot remember is gone for good, they thought.

Since then I have walked about expounding my idea to anyone who will listen, but there are very few who understand what I mean. Are we becoming so materialistic that we find our *pictures* more important than our dream images? Is our culture so saturated with pictures that it has become dream-poor? We must be watching too much television and too many videos. Or am I talking to the wrong people? I hope so.

104

Ego Types

The dream image is no picture. It is not an *Abbild,* to use the German. That is, it is not derived from anything else; it is not a video image that one can watch, it is not a picture that you can hold in your hand and consult from time to time when in need of a true love. And it is absolutely not an extract or an abstraction.

If you try to describe or depict your dream image, you will find that it really is not possible. Or you are forced to resort to images and make an image of an image. Or you come with a list of individual characteristics that usually sooner reveal what you do not want than what you do want.

That is no wonder. A dream image is, after all, an image from a dream. But it is not a shadow or a phantom; it is far too familiar for that. It knows our deepest thoughts and is very close to us.

It is the dream lover that the ego has imagined and for whom it longs. And yet the image dissolves in a mist for those who do not dream and reach out toward it.

Even those who do not reach out toward it are unconsciously aware of it in their day-to-day lives. Thus from time to time they are struck by someone's appearance, which evokes a feeling of recognition of the dream image. It happens more frequently with some than with others. Most have no recognition whatsoever, even when they look long and hard. (But nothing comes of true recognition if one has become the victim of delusion. In this case, they either never recognize anyone, or they think that they recognize everyone.)

People with appearances that evoke our recognition (excluding our delusions, of course) are located within the parameters of our ego type. That is significantly smaller than our erotic type and usually lies completely within the latter. In other, less complicated, words, Eros w.d. can enjoy a night of lovemaking with many, but Narcissus is more selective when searching among the many for someone whom he can really get along with.

"Where?"

The opening of an old pick-up line is not so crazy after all. A boy sees something in an unfamiliar girl, walks up to her, and recites the following script: "Haven't we met somewhere before?" When she asks, with raised eyebrows, "Where?" his answer should be, "In our world of imagination. We were already crazy about each other when we were little children. We played hide-and-go-seek under the stars of the Milky Way and hunted for mysterious, gleaming pearls on the bottom of the mother ocean."

If he says all that, she will either immediately be struck by him, or she will laugh in his face. But he will not say it. He will begin to stutter and to lie. Then she will not deem him worthy of another glance, and that is too bad, because with further and deeper examination the recognition could be mutual.

Being Struck

Whether or not it actually comes to the point of recognition is hit or miss. You can only hope to come across someone with an appearance that can be located somewhere near the center of your ego type. That is where the greatest possible mutual recognition occurs. The "mutual" part is important, but the "greatest possible" is no less important. If it is not the "greatest possible," there remains a certain longing for someone else. It then comes to expression in the continual attempt to *force* one's beloved to conform *completely* in appearance to the dream image. That is never entirely possible and provokes deep resistance.

Another consequence can be that at the most unexpected moments one gets the feeling of being in love. This feeling can be compared with those that surround erotic fascination. That is because we regularly meet people who belong to our ego type. We are then struck by something of the image recognition.

If one already has a true love, nothing further happens. At most, the thought arises: "Nice person, just my type." But if one has a forced love, the desire for completeness can surface. "Could this be everything I've been looking for?" Then the forced love is continued with twice the effort, or being struck is confused with being in love.

The same can occur, almost without notice, during problem periods in the we-covenant. For that reason it is of primary importance to devote attention to the problem.

Dreaming Together

What happens to the dream images of two lovers who have found their ego type and have nothing more to hope for, *nor desire to hope for more?*

The answer is that their dream images have been removed from the world of imagination and have been made a reality. From then on they dream together in order to make their dream a reality together. That is one of the many ways in which the fire of love is provided with new fuel.

Choosing

Before things actually get that far, one must begin by making a *choice*. Mirror and image point to ego experiences. But the *responsibility* of Narcissus does not yet appear in the myth.

It was simply something that happened to Ovid's Narcissus. The modern Narcissus does not get off so easily. Narcissus wants a partner for his ego, so he must choose.

Will he open up the deep accesses so that the heart can be reached and we can speak of true love? Or will he choose not to do so? Does he want a relationship-contract but not a we-covenant? Or does he just want sex? Or a relationship without sex?

In each of the latter cases, he remains Narcissus w.d., and moves beyond the boundaries of love.

But it is not, per se, an objective choice, at least if he is candid and forthright with the other. That must emphatically be part of the equation, since it is often lacking.

The Buffet

John is unable or unwilling to choose. He himself said that he does not want to (yet), but I suspect that he is not able to. Because in order to choose, a certain ego strength is necessary; call it the ability to assume freedom and responsibility. Those who choose honestly weigh all the pros and cons and then come down on one side or the other. In this way they give a certain shape to their lives; they choose their own path, to the exclusion of others.

John says that where women are concerned, he likes, for the time being, the buffet approach. One walks about licking one's lips and sampling the fares, putting a little of this and a little of that on one's plate, leisurely consuming one's meal, and then starting over with a clean plate and trying something completely different. *Varietas delectat.* Variety is the spice of life.

In so doing he behaves as the consummate representative of the consumer society. Narcissus w.d. can, as noted, be nothing other than a consumer. He is completely dependent on the market, on what is available and on the attractiveness of the display.

The fool calls that dependence "freedom." He is unable to fathom that human *freedom* consists precisely in assuming *responsibility*, in the making of choices.

But the despicable thing about his conduct is that he is not entirely honest with the women with whom he consorts. He suggests by his conduct that something could really come of it, when in fact he already has in mind what he is going to have on his plate next time around. In the meantime, he lets them dance to his tune, as long as he finds them pleasing.

It is still completely unclear to me why there are still women who fall into his trap, when they themselves want nothing of the buffet.

Ego-Love

Self-love still has a bad name. If you speak of it in a positive fashion, you immediately receive the rebuke that it fosters egoism. Self-love is not true love, they continually and uncritically say. True love is self-sacrificial, makes the self of no account, and desires good for the other, not for itself.

I find these observations incorrect. We met them earlier in another form, with Rita and the woman in the bathrobe. It is my opinion that self-love is necessary in order to be able to love another. On this insight hang the whole law and the prophets. For practical reasons I will exchange the term self-love for ego-love. It makes no difference regarding the definiteness of my assertion: *whoever does not love his ego is not able to love another either.* It simply is not possible. Just consider those people who are always at loose ends. They all have problems loving. The reverse is just as true. Whoever is unable to love another does not love himself. He may deceive himself, but he knows it is true.

Now the term can be more closely defined: ego-love is something like dealing with oneself on the basis of a positive self-consciousness, of *self-respect.* In other words, a person must treat herself with respect for her basic nature and insist that others do so as well. This point of view immediately provokes traditional questions about limits. There are none.

"I'm here too!" Narcissus rightly calls out. His ego is there, but by the grace of being-other. Certainly.

There are no limits, but there are essential conditions. The most important is still that the heart be engaged. Ego-love opens up the deep access to the heart. Where that is not so, the dangers of egoism, consumerism, and narcissism lurk just around the corner. But we will get to that later.

A Covenant with the Self

Narcissus now stands in front of his own mirror and looks deeply. He looks through the reflecting surface — yes, he! — and even through the cracks that criss-cross the mosaic of his own nature. More deeply Narcissus cannot look; Shulamite can, but she is not yet in sight.

For the time being, Narcissus looks deeply enough. Before he does anything with love, he must first make a covenant with himself. He must resolutely pledge to love himself and to remain faithful to himself, because what he sees there in the depths is a person who is well worthy of love. Narcissus may not distance himself from that fact. On the contrary, he must try to come as close to it as possible. That gives him the courage to go further, against the tide. "If I die, I die, but I will not surrender my ego. I will fight for it — with myself and with every *force and overwhelming power* that attempts to alienate me from myself!"

Those who look deeply in their own mirrors and do not see an image that inspires them are not able to love. Lonely, dependent, and bitter people, for example, must first restore their self-respect and with it their ego-love, before they attempt to begin anything.

109

The lonely must first learn (again) to be alone, *because whoever is not able to be alone will have problems living with others.*

The dependent must learn to care for themselves, *because whoever cannot care for himself cannot care for others.*

The bitter must come to terms with their past and therefore also with their future, *because whoever is at odds with her own past is not prepared for a new future.*

Past-Imperfect Tense

Nick left his wife. Why he did so is not entirely clear to him. "It just wasn't working anymore," he said vaguely. "I don't think we ever loved each other."

The more I speak with him, the less believable that seems to me. As far as I am concerned, he has not acknowledged that his problems are solvable. But sometimes such cases are hard to turn around. The idiot has too hastily made a number of irreversible decisions.

Now Nick is bitter. His self-respect is completely gone. He has not only left his beloved for dubious reasons, but his children no longer accept him, he never sees his dog anymore, and the other things that were part of his life are for the most part beyond his reach. Nick has lost a large number of the things to which his ego was attached.

And so he is grieving, attempting to free himself from that growing sense of bitterness, trying to come clean with himself so that self-respect and ego-love are possible again. Not hiding anything and trying to put an end to the past-imperfect tense to make it past-perfect tense. He must do all that, *at least if he wants to move forward.*

And so he does, gladly, but not along the only available path. He is foolish enough to believe that *an other* can fill up the void of his ego-loss. And so he falls immediately into the arms and the bed of Marie.

But if he should ever overcome his bitterness, which under these circumstances is still an open question, he will not need Marie anymore. To her then falls the same lot as the therapy-practicing female students. She will be completely broken up by it all, but she should have known. There is no future in love with someone who has not come to terms with his past.

But it never gets to that point. Marie also has a thing or two in her past that still possess her.

In fact they have both abandoned love, even though they do not say so out loud. *Without consciously making the decision,* they make a mutually beneficial contract, in the vague hope of getting on with things. But she continues to nurture her hatred for her ex-husband, and he remains bitter about his ego-loss.

That way, at least, they have plenty to talk about, and they get on manageably well.

Perhaps there is nothing more in it for them. Two persons, bruised by life, with a lack of ego-love. Sometimes, someone is better than no one and something is better than nothing.

Whoever is *unable* to look deep in his own mirror is immature. Whoever is *unwilling* is irresponsible. Both are forms of ego-weakness. Such people should expect nothing from love.

Can I Do This? Do I Choose To?

In the realm of the ego we find not just mirrors into which one can or cannot look deeply, and images that may or may not strike one. It is also the realm of *choosing,* as we have stated.

There are a number of decisions that Narcissus cannot avoid unless he wants to deprive his ego. Moreover, he must be able to open his heart without threat of danger. Thus he does himself a favor by creating a little clarity concerning what it is that he does and does not want.

Even though we may belong completely to each other's erotic type, and even though we may find ourselves — complete with first-rate mirrors — in the dead center of each other's ego type, it is still possible that in our day-to-day life we are unsuited for each other.

That depends on both our *circumstances,* both our *worlds of meaning,* and both our *worlds of experience.* For they can be so distant from each other that we do well to consider whether it is indeed wise to continue together.

"Can I do this? Do I choose to do this? Do I really want this?" If these questions are not posed by Narcissus from the outset, they will return in another form. Then it is too late to choose freely. Then it is, "Did I really choose that? Did I actually want that then?"

In order to be able to choose, a person must of course first know what she is able to do and what she wants to do. The unfortunate thing about love is that many people are unable to do what they want and unwilling to do what they are able. That brings us to repentance and self-knowledge.

During that seventh-heaven feeling that results from having been struck by each other, few people take the time to reflect. They go head over heels through the door under the motto, "We'll take care of all that other stuff later. This is so unbelievably wonderful, no one can take this away from us."

This is also a choice. But when the ship of love appears to go aground, we ought not complain to each other or blame each other.

Is it "better to have loved and lost than never to have loved at all"? Yes, I think so. But the grounding of the ship often goes hand in hand with irreparable damage: disappointment, ego-loss. These can be corrected, but a broken heart, that is serious. "Look before you leap, then you won't have to repent later." That was my wise, moralistic old grandmother again.

An Aside

The free choice of a lifelong partner has not occurred in all times and all places. Who belongs with whom has been, and still is, sometimes determined by others — for example, in cultures where marriage is viewed as a contract between two families. But there are also others who concern themselves with such matters.

"Liking each other and being struck by each other is very nice, but being right for each other is even better — and that is something that can better be judged by others than by you," is one of the assumptions that lie behind such actions.

Such statements make modern, individualized people downright angry. They decide for them*selves* what is good for them. They do not need their parents, or the priest, or the community leader for that.

Good enough, and yet I often see that they do not so much decide for themselves as let circumstances overtake them, without daring to give their life any particular shape. There are even those who do not dare choose a career. They give that responsibility to a career training office. Choose a partner? No thank you.

The Patriarch

In Drenthe, the Netherlands, they still tell stories about an old patriarchal factory owner whose workers had to ask his permission in order to marry off their children. If he did not like the arrangement, it did not happen. Those who opposed him were fired along with their whole family.

A new pastor had the audacity to speak to him about it. To everyone's surprise, he was not thrown out on his ear. He was cooly told that the textile workers were too stupid to understand that not just any man could get along with just any woman. The patriarch knew his people better than they knew themselves, and therefore he sometimes felt it his duty to protect them against their own better judgment. And the pastor who had just come and did not have a damn clue about "circumstances," "worlds of meaning," and "worlds of experience" was politely asked not to concern himself further with such matters. (That last part was of course not said in so many words, but it boiled down to the same thing.)

Modern people no longer allow such patriarchs to choose for them. *But they ought not neglect to do it themselves,* because otherwise the old ogre will prove to be right — and I am not prepared to grant him that.

Those who do not take "circumstances," "worlds of meaning," and "worlds of experience" into account in love and fail to choose self-consciously run a high risk of sooner or later having to make an appointment with the modern descendants of the patriarch: the therapist.

Michael Again

"Michael, the moment has arrived to speak further with you. You spoke to me at the beginning about love being like a kerosene lamp, inefficient, with the awful smell of soot. Remember?

"At that time, I still took you seriously. But not anymore. I see through you now. You are a foolish, conniving little rat. You have always mistaken the circumstances that lay before you for an independent judgment.

"Circumstances? You have never let them affect you. You were above them. Think ahead, make choices? You just reflexively followed along with whatever happened to occur to you. You knew very well that those two nice women would not fit into your circumstances. But you took a chance on them anyway. You promised them golden mountains, but you had no intentions of changing anything. And so it fell apart. Twice.

"Now you are all miserable. Three adults and four children."

And what does Michael do? He does not hit himself over the head until the plate cracks. No, Michael, who has squandered his chances for love, is still arrogant enough to announce everywhere that true love does not exist and never existed. The problem is not with him, he yells, the problem is with love: "an inefficient oil lamp with the awful smell of soot." What you say is what you are.

"I will still listen to the others, but I will no longer listen to you."

Circumstances

Let us return again to the main line of thought.

Narcissus — the love-seeking ego — is responsible for the choices he makes, or does not make.

A lover's desire and longing are for someone. The erotic, mirrors, image; everything is perfectly and mutually present — that we know. Does she also choose his circumstances, the facts of his existence?

Some are unchangeable. Just to give two examples of a very different nature: there are children to be brought up. There is a job that frequently requires lengthy absences. Other circumstances can change suddenly, and for that reason introduce an element of chaos into an existing we-covenant. The business is failing and the income drops precipitously. "I did not choose that!" But now what?

"Completely normal," Beck and Beck-Gernsheim say. But they are sociologists and therefore think that circumstances determine the person. We will speak more of them later.

Some circumstances are perhaps purposely changed, but in that regard Narcissus easily errs.

There Already Is Someone

There is, for example, already someone in the life of the man on whom she has set her sights. That can be a circumstance that is quickly re-medied. But the ease with which that happens then creates a new cir-cumstance that she does not necessarily want to choose.

Naturally, the man has a good story that she really wants to believe. But the fact remains, even though it is difficult for outsiders to understand.

More believably, however, "the other" is not at all that easy to get rid of.

The man does not want to. He does not want to hurt the children, he wants to remain "faithful," they have gone through too much together already, it would be bad for his career — that kind of chatter. Or worse, he keeps her on the line, promises her that he will make work of it, but does nothing.

When she says that she cannot take it anymore, and thus does not choose this, she must then either send him away or deny him access to her heart, because otherwise, in the long run, she will run into grave difficulties. But like the choice of Narcissus, she must remain true to herself and do nothing that will cause her to despise herself and to suffer from a lack of self-respect and ego-love. For in that case, she would be temporarily indisposed for true love.

But even if the man is willing and able quickly to take formal steps to distance himself from the other, it is still the case that the other is not in fact gone. She undoubtedly still plays a role in his world of meaning and his world of experience, as was the case with Nick and Marie.

The fact of the existence of the other also remains. That is what it is all about here. No one can silently close the door of a bedroom. The inevitable aftermath is an accompanying circumstance that is not to be removed by cuddling on the couch with a glass of wine. And so one must create clarity and choose. They cannot be separated.

Overwhelming Power

There are innumerable imaginable circumstances that require reflection and choice.

"Can I do this?" That is a necessary and fair question. A number of dramatic stories occur to me in this regard, which seem to indicate that there are times when this question may not be asked, due to the overwhelming power of circumstances.

Condemned by Circumstances to . . .

They were not yet twenty and already had, how should we say . . . "a friendship, a relationship," as they themselves put it. A casual relationship, we used to say. But it was the first serious relationship for both of them.

They had immediately begun to experiment sexually with much enthusiasm. Perhaps it was even investment-erotic.

Actually things did not go all that well. She asked herself from time to time whether she really wanted to stay with him. On the one hand he was still such a child, and on the other hand such a dominating ogre. But he was good looking, and whenever she was sitting next to him in the car or lying beside him in bed, she forgot all her doubts.

Half of her friends advised her to cut things off immediately, while the other half told her she should wait with a decision.

And so she waited. Until, after a night of drinking, they drove off the road. She escaped with a broken collarbone, but he had spinal injuries and a concussion. Suddenly she had no more choices and was condemned by circumstances to care for him.

116

She was immediately thought by everyone to be an absolute angel, the only one who could pull him through it all, the self-sacrificial lover who would never, never abandon him. Isn't it wonderful? She would never leave her lover stranded in a wheelchair.

Doctors took her into their confidence, his father and mother clung to her. Her own parents were painfully proud of her. Everyone assumed that their love was forever.

I asked her, "Are you up to this? Do you choose this?"

She looked at me, bewildered. The heroine role, with all the accompanying admiration? Sure, that was great. Her father asked me what the hell I was after. Nothing? Well, it had better stay that way.

That was about ten years ago. They were married, and she is utterly unhappy. He is still a child and a dominating ogre, and the latter has only gotten worse because his disability has placed him above all criticism.

"You're healthy and I'm handicapped, so you must blindly obey me. Your wishes don't interest me, because you're healthy and I . . ." etc. The whole damn day.

The investment-erotic and experimental sex is all gone. She groans under his demands. But she is chained to him, not by bonds of love, but by unforeseen circumstances, which prevent her from thinking about herself. I find that very sad.

"Should she not have allowed her heart to have its say after that accident?"

"Her heart? She had not yet gotten that far. Nor did she let it speak. She simply did what circumstances demanded of her. Her ego did not even have the chance to make a choice; not then and not now. Nothing enters the heart that is not first in (the senses and) the ego."

In order to avoid misunderstanding, we must immediately add another story to this one, which will point to the next chapter. Because in love, at a given moment, *choice passes over into decision,* in the devotion of the heart. Then everything changes.

Short but Very Sweet

They had been married nearly thirty years when the last of their four daughters left the house. The next phase, that of the "empty nest," was a bit difficult for Nelle, as was to be expected. But together they finally came through it well, and began to take pleasure in new, unexpected horizons.

Then she was diagnosed with cancer — of the slow, insidious, "fear-and-hope" kind. Slowly, very slowly, she went from being a vivacious woman to being but a remote caricature of herself.

He, Herman, died a thousand deaths, but stayed on his feet for her, even when she was dead and buried.

It was years before he was able to sleep without a nightlight and was almost over the nightmares in which he relived it all, even worse than before.

His daughters were anxious for him to look for "a new partner," as they put it. When he thought that his life with Nelle had become past-perfect tense, he had to make a choice. "Can I do this? Do I really want to?" Yes.

He was not altogether sure how it would fit in with his work, and so there were a couple of misses. His daughters were also unknowingly in part to blame for that, because they really wanted to arrange things for their old dad and continually came up with the most improbable women, who fell well beyond his type.

He had already become disenchanted when Lisa appeared. Bull's-eye! Everything was perfect. "Things just clicked immediately," his daughters said. Herman and Lisa asked themselves and each other the question that Narcissus must ask himself: Can I do this? Do I want to? Yes.

Then they had to see if they were really right for each other, because a person can be badly mistaken about himself and about the other.

After five wonderful weeks of intensive companionship, Lisa was found to have cancer, more or less of the same nasty type as Nelle. She immediately returned home and wanted nothing further to do with him.

"She's right," I said. "You don't have to go through this again. Your old grief will immediately be reactivated, and you will no longer be able to tell who Nelle is and who Lisa is. You are not up to this, you don't really want this. You did not choose this."

"You are right," he said. "But that is not the issue. You can always come back to a choice, albeit in circumstances of extreme need. But *I am an eternity beyond choice. For three weeks already.* I made the decision; I have devoted my heart to her. I love her. That is very different.

"If she also loves me — and I think she does — she will agree that we should go on together. Already a month ago we talked about getting married. We should do it then, shouldn't we?"

Such a man is not sacrificing himself, not at all. He is simply being true to himself and is doing what he cannot avoid: loving his beloved.

"But it will ruin you, Herman," I still tried.

"Maybe," he said. "If I die, then I die. Just as long as we can be together until death do us part."

(He did not say it quite so precisely. But again, that is what it boiled down to.)

They were married in all glory, as though they had a lifetime in front of them. And so it was.

But she was soon bedridden. And their life together was short, but very sweet.

Asymmetrical Circumstances

Love can prosper even when the partners are very different, but not easily. It can only succeed if they have individually and together reflected in depth on the Narcissus questions, and then have made their choice.

Asymmetrical circumstances can add to love an exciting, enriching, venturous dimension, but there are and remain risk factors.

Some of the situations that come to mind are large differences in age, energy, background, class, status, and cultural factors, such as religion, art, politics, vocation, language, hobbies, cleanliness and clothing, and eating and drinking habits. The way in which the other is embedded in a social or family system also calls for choices.

A number of these facts can be changed, if it is so desired. Language and eating habits, for example. But others cannot be changed, and therefore they must at least be tolerated. Or not.

Some can be carried on separately within the love relationship — for example, when one has a great deal of energy and the other is not physically capable. Then they must act separately; nothing can be done about that. "Tell me all about it when you get home. I would love to hear about it!"

But Narcissus is not only looking to share a bed. There must be enough common overlap. That demands, in certain situations of extreme asymmetry, a certain *adaptation*. Who must adapt, and to what point? Who must make the compromise?

Then the Narcissus questions arise again. *If they are not posed and answered, they will with time pose and answer themselves.* But there are other, deeper questions. The first is that of the world of meaning.

An Aside

Is it really a question of love, or am I actually simply providing a rationale for socially acceptable behavior, "for mutual benefit"?

Yes, it is still a question of love, of a total, authentic love covenant. And so *nothing is left out of the equation.* On the contrary, everything enters into the equation. All systems go, full speed ahead! Left and right hand. Senses, ego, and heart.

But right now, in this chapter, we are talking about Narcissus and ego-love. Narcissus must reflect, he must weigh and choose. That is not simply rational; it is an act of self-consciousness. To be sure, not of the whole self-consciousness, but that will come. First half speed, then full speed ahead.

World of Meaning

The Narcissus questions concern not only the circumstances, but also the world of meaning. Here we are dealing not with the facts of the other's existence, but the meaning that is attached to them. What is the *importance* of those facts; what *place* do they occupy in the life of the beloved?

One has, for example, a sea-going sailboat, and the other a fear of water. Those are circumstances. Change? Do things separately? Adapt? That depends on what that boat and sailing mean in that person's life. Is it of peripheral or of *central importance?*

The latter is the case if the woman (or man) has derived a good part of her self-respect and individuality from sailing. It can be something to which she is so attached that she experiences ego-loss if it disappears from her life.

Then we can only hope that the other does not develop a real aversion to it. ("Just shut up. I don't even want to talk about it!") Acting separately within the love relationship is under these circumstances impossible, because the sailor is completely involved while the one who fears water delivers highly cynical commentary. And so it has to be kept out of the love relationship. That is possible, but it is very dangerous. *Couples have to be able actively or passively to share central meanings,* or at least be able to tolerate them. If that is not the case, one must seriously consider whether one really is willing and able. I also know of cases where suddenly, after many years, just like that the one enters into an area of meaning that is not only entirely foreign to the other, but to which the other has a real aversion. ("He has never been seen near a dog and suddenly I have two of the rats in my house and he spends all day Saturday at the kennel club. He has gone crazy over them. Should I just accept that?")

Whoever does such a thing must be fully aware that love is at risk. One cannot within the love relationship develop with impunity a central meaning that the other would never have chosen.

But why not? Human existence consists of an infinite number of areas in which to immerse oneself. Must precisely the one be chosen that creates the alienation of the beloved?

Sandra Again

Unfortunately, that sometimes is the case. I am thinking of Sandra, who became interested in the women's movement and then discovered that her husband was in no condition or was not prepared to even listen to what she had to say.

"And you got involved in all this in order to increase the

pressure? You suddenly want to change everything and not talk about it anymore?"

Now she is mad. "Of course you would take his side. You are all like that. No man is in a position to understand what a woman feels."

"But could you not have taken things a bit more slowly? You knew that you were rubbing against the grain. Does the women's movement really mean that much to you? Or are you just looking for a good alibi to get rid of him with a clean conscience?"

They are hard questions. But a person should not just step out of the way when love is at stake.

Later she comes back to it.

"I think that he has driven me into a corner," she says, "and that his behavior just convinced me all the more that I was right. Then I became a changed woman and he said that I was not the person he had chosen. And then he had an affair with my twin sister, the slut."

"Completely normal," the Beck sisters would say again, but I find it sad. Fortunately it can turn out completely different as well. But not without an investment.

The more meaning that is shared, the greater the chances of stability in the relationship. *They do not have to be the same, but it is imperative that they be able to enter into dialogue with each other.* Then they enrich each other. That is what I mean by having access to the other's world of meaning.

World of Experience

The Narcissus questions are also applicable to the access to the other's world of experience. That is, *the configuration of deep accesses whereby the heart of the other can be reached.* It is a very personal, intimate, vulnerable realm. One cannot just let anyone have access to it. But the beloved has free access to it, by definition.

We are not going to talk again here about one-handed people like Thomas. They are, like sacrificial victims of the technological world, condemned to a life without true love. At best, there may still be something to offer him in the realm of Eros or Narcissus, but then the w.d. narcissism of Lasch becomes a real threat.

Even less do we want to speak again of those miserable people who very early on were forced to protect their heart with defenses.

We are dealing now with the normal, everyday person for whom the full self-conscious is in principle easily accessible: all systems go, full speed ahead, all systems engaged and integrated: senses, ego, and heart.

Under what circumstances does that happen? What is meaningful for his heart? How can he be touched? What moves him? The answer to these questions makes it fairly clear how his world of experience looks *from the outside*. Narcissus must experience that as quickly as possible. But that is not enough, not nearly enough. Can she really enter into the world of experience of the other, and *be* herself there?

If the answer to this very essential question is unknown, she would do well not to begin anything, or to stop what she has done immediately, no matter what. *Because if there is little or nothing to experience together, there is also little or nothing to love.*

Making love, as long as it lasts? The comfort of a companion? Sharing meaning? Granted, that is a lot. But love, commitment through thick and thin . . . that requires a common world of experience.

Believing

Circumstances can change dramatically and a person's world of meaning can suddenly collapse. All that was meaningful, everything that had value, suddenly appears useless. Not only preferences, opinions, and points of view, but also world and life views.

It leaves a person at a complete loss; unsteady on the shaky ground of the fragility of existence. "Why was I ever born?" That can occur, for example, when out of the clear blue a child commits suicide, or when one receives the unexpected news that a beloved one does not have long to live.

The experience that remains — after everything else falls away — that is what a person truly believes, at the bottom of her heart.

I would never dare to enter a relationship with someone who could not share that experience.

If the answer to the very essential question regarding the access to the world of experience is ambiguous, things will be difficult. Make an attempt? Maybe it will work out? Benefit of the doubt? Can I do this? Do I want this?

I myself am inclined to say, "In dubiis abstine," or "When in doubt, do nothing." Shulamite agrees with me on that one: "Do not force love, you cannot awaken love until it so desires."

Those who are ready for love, however, are frequently prepared to take all kinds of risks. They do not hold back in cases of doubt, but rather try all the harder. Everyone must take their lumps.

But do not, then, make superficial statements about love if things go wrong.

Zeke Again

That last comment was intended for Zeke, who talked in the beginning about an unbridgeable generation gap.

He is a naively optimistic man who has stayed with his mother too long. When she died, he built a very unique world of experience — romantic, mystical, and artistic. Everything very nice and vague, light green and soft rose colored.

Actually he cannot yet imagine that not everyone is just like him. Since he is a gentle, friendly man, he is much admired by certain women, who typically are much younger than himself.

Every time the relationship seemed somewhat empty where type and circumstances were concerned, he simply assumed that things would still be all right with the world of meaning and the world of experience. And so time after time things fell apart, and he lost his courage.

He saves face now by making superficial statements about love. "The gap that separates us is too great to be bridged. Love is the most individual expression of the most individual emotion. No one understands my heart, but I can't cry about that. My mother's generation and culture, they understood what love was. But today. . . . Ah, what does it matter."

I find such talk destructive and unnecessary. Because she is out there, the woman with whom he could be "utterly and completely happy." She is out there, and love is too. She is from all times and in all places. "Zeke, you're a nice guy, but I will no longer listen to you if you continue to talk so condescendingly about love."

Drip Valve

In the laboratory where I used to work a large glass funnel sat on a tripod with a tapered nozzle at the end of which was a small drip valve.

Is that the way to find love? A large funnel with a drip valve? One might even believe it. The upper part, that of the erotic type, is very wide. That of the ego-type is narrower. Yet narrower is the part of the mirrors. The nozzle, finally, contains the select, refined space of, world of meaning, and world of experience.

Have we arrived? Then the valve may be opened. Love drips out. And that is that. The drip valve.

But that is not the way it is. What we said above is all true — as far as I can see — but finding true love cannot be represented by the analogy of the funnel. It is not even a process of selection or refinement, as though one could carry out the search with the help of a checklist of demands and desires.

"Madam/Sir, we regret to have to inform you that you were not our first choice. With your permission, we will keep your application on file, for future reference. With kindest regards, etc." (And I am not just making this up. Not entirely at least.)

The Marvel of the Spark

Even if love were to be played out in the realm of the senses and the ego, even then, it could not be done on the basis of this selection process.

Eros *reacts reflexively.* He himself does not even know why. Narcissus is *struck by an image,* which he cannot even describe or depict.

125

But that is nothing compared to the *marvel of the spark*. Because even when everything fits perfectly between two people — Eros and Narcissus, types, mirrors, circumstances, meaning, deep accesses, and whatever else one can imagine — that does not mean that they will still love each other.

Choices are necessary, decisions inevitable. But love is also a fire. A fire that must be lit by a spark. That wonderful spark that sets aflame heart and soul and strength and mind.

Now we have arrived at love as a marvel and as a gift that is given. Shulamite knows all about it.

8. Shulamite

It has taken a long time — too long — before we could talk about Shulamite. First we had to say everything there was to say about Eros and Narcissus. We ought not assume from that, however, that they have priority over her; on the contrary. Nor is it the case that they can share with us anything that this woman does not already possess; once again, on the contrary.

The reason we began with them is twofold. In the first place, under the influence of Hellenism, Shulamite has been removed from our daily lives and has been hidden away, exiled to the sacred realm of the Mount of the Sublime. They pray there, but they do not make love, and ego-love is frowned upon.

Thus if one begins too quickly with Shulamite and agape[1] — that is, true love — one runs the risk of being misunderstood. That is the second reason we began by giving Eros and Narcissus their due: they both play a very influential role in the Western world of experience where ordinary love is concerned. Most people know them by name and nickname, but you cannot say that about Shulamite.

---

1. It is really an anachronism to speak of agape in connection with the Song of Solomon, since it is a Greek term whose content is Christian. For that reason, Kristeva prefers the Hebrew term *ahav,* while in Decker-Dijs we still find agape. In order not to make things too complicated, I will follow the latter example. In retrospect the choice is defensible.

Messianic

Actually we don't know her real name. And that is why she is properly called Shulamite, the woman from Shulam, but it could also be Shunam. It does not seem to matter much.

In my opinion, *she is the most important woman in the history of humankind*,[2] because she grants true love the place it deserves. According to the book of Genesis, something went very wrong with love in the Garden of Eden. Cracks appeared in the mosaic which cause us suffering even today.

In the garden of Shulamite, it is clear from her actions that the cracks do not form part of the pattern of the mosaic, and that things could be very different. And how! That is why I see her as the messianic woman *par excellence*. Yet how she has been misconstrued by Hellenism and beaten about! Thank God, a sort of reevaluation has begun lately in feminist theology. It is high time.

Her poetry can be found in the Bible. The Old Testament contains a small work that was called "shir ha shirim," which means something like Song of Songs. Under the influence of various English translations of the Bible, it came to be known as the Song of Solomon.

In the Jewish tradition it is read on the eighth day of the feast of the exodus from slavery, *pesach*, or Passover. Obviously, the rabbis detect something messianic in the book.

Assurance and Hope

It is truly surprising how much can be found in the Song of Songs about true love. Those who give it a naive reading, like I do, will perceive something of that love. And those who give it a close reading move from

2. And Mary, then? The Madonna? The glorious focal point of the Maesta? I have diligently sought the *woman* in her *but have not been able to find her.* Not in mariology, not in the literature, sometimes in the paintings, but then again not. She was even less in Lourdes and Fatima; not when I was there at least.

Miriam, the mother of Jesus, the innocent Jewish girl with the ineffable religious experience that she hid in her heart — I know her very well. But she is far too modest to want to be the most important woman in all of history.

Stabat Mater, the downcast, mourning mother — I know her even better. She is the woman of the Pietas.

one chill-inspiring moment to the next.[3] Compared to the Song of Songs, even the compositions of Bach appear to be simple, pedantic works.

Why am I so interested in this book? Because this feminine poetry seems to me to be the most suitable form for illuminating love. Imaginative and therefore visionary; musical and therefore direct; symbolic and therefore puzzling; revealing, concealing, and ambiguous.

"It is a treasure chest, to which we have lost the key," the great Saadya said regarding the Song of Songs about A.D. 900.[4] It seems to me that only in the last twenty years have we begun seeking seriously in the right direction again.

From her poetry, Shulamite arises before us as the *equal, intiative-taking, loving lover.*

From out of a deeply integrated unity (individuality, indivisibility) of senses, ego, and heart — desiring, longing, and yearning — she devotes herself, *deciding* between life and death, dialogically with her beloved, whom she loves "as such" and not for any other reason.

When she wants to possess him, he seems to flee, although they both know that they belong to each other. The most beautiful part is yet to come. She knows it too. That happy future that on them shines, makes them restless and excited. *You have been given to me, I found you, but I must continue to seek you.*

Hiddenness and anticipation, assurance, and anxious, wonderful hope. Love is the most poetic form of living. Here you are, right next to me. And yet you are also far away. Do you still love me? Is it really true? It is almost too beautiful to be true. Tell me again where I can find what has been given to me over and over again.

Exclusive and Radiating

Such a total, intensive, ardent devotion can never be anything other than *exclusive between two people,* because the "nephesh," the soul, the warmth of the blood, the heart is indivisible.

Eros w.d. may desire many; Narcissus w.d. may long for the com-

---

3. See Decker-Dijs.

4. Saadya (892-942) was a famous Jewish scholar. Cf. L. Browne, *The Wisdom of Israel* (London, 1949).

panionship of a number of others. In Shulamite, desire and longing reach the heart. There they are fused into indivisible love, true love, agape, the love that overtakes us.

By love's impulse, Shulamite yearns for only one person. Sometimes she calls him king, because she knows that she is a queen. More often she calls him "My lover." You and I, we together. My everything.

Her beloved says it too: You are my everything, my beloved, my bride, my friend, my sister! What would he want with anyone else, when she is his everything?

Shulamite cannot do it for less, even though she is sometimes frightened by the prospect. All or nothing. She assumes the risk that she might lose everything and have nothing left over.

Whoever loves in this way can be nothing other than monogomous, withdrawn, and jealous.

And precisely therein her love radiates outward. Lovers are the image of God. All of reality participates in love; as image and as related to it. People, animals, plants, things. Wind, fire, water, and earth. God.

No trace of the obscure here. Only clear, clear, clear! The garden of Shulamite is the Garden of Gardens in the Land of Love, the restoration of the Garden of Eden, with a view of the Garden of Gethsemane, a foretaste of the Kingdom.

Your Love Is Sweeter than Wine

Like all poetry, her poetry must be read openly and in its entirety. If possible, together with one's beloved. Right next to each other. With wine, candlelight, and incense. They can take turns reading: the words of the one, the words of the other, the words of the others together. In this way the experience of the poetry is complete. (One can later give it a technical reading by the light of a halogen lamp, if so desired, in order to delve even more deeply.)

Just to pique the curiosity, here are a few verses — a personal selection, which can only give an incomplete impression.[5]

5. From the Dutch *Grote Nieuws Bijbel* (Boxtel, Haarlem, 1983); English translation based on the NIV. Where the two texts differ significantly, the Dutch text has been followed.

Beloved:

> Let him kiss me with the kisses of his mouth—
> for your love is more delightful than wine.
> Pleasing is the fragrance of your perfumes;
> your name is like perfume poured out.
> No wonder the maidens love you!
> Take me away with you—let us hurry!
> Let the king bring me into his chambers.

Friends:

> We rejoice and delight in you;
> We will praise your love more than wine.   *(2:1-7)*

Beloved:

> I am a rose of Sharon,
> a lily of the valleys.

Lover:

> Like a lily among thorns is my darling among the maidens.

Beloved:

> Like an apple tree among the trees of the forest
> is my lover among the young men.
> I delight to sit in his shade,
> and his fruit is sweet to my taste.
> He has taken me to the banquet hall,
> and his banner over me is love.
> Strengthen me with raisins,
> refresh me with apples,
> for I am faint with love.
> His left arm is under my head,
> and his right arm embraces me.
> Daughters of Jerusalem, I charge you

by the gazelles and by the does of the field:
Do not arouse or awaken love until it so desires. *(1:2-4)*

Lover:

You have stolen my heart, my sister, my bride;
you have stolen my heart with one glance of your eyes,
with one jewel of your necklace.
How delightful is your love, my sister, my bride!
How much more pleasing is your love than wine,
and the fragrance of your perfume than any spice!
Your lips drop sweetness as the honeycomb, my bride;
milk and honey are under your tongue.
The fragrance of your garments is like that of Lebanon.
You are a garden locked up, my sister, my bride;
you are a spring enclosed, a sealed fountain.
Your plants are an orchard of pomegranates,
with choice fruits, with henna and nard,
nard and saffron, calamus and cinnamon,
with every kind of incense tree,
with myrrh and aloes and all the finest spices.
You are a garden fountain,
a well of flowing water streaming down from Lebanon.

(4:9-15)

Beloved:

I slept but my heart was awake.
Listen! My lover is knocking:
"Open to me, my sister, my darling, my flawless one.
My head is drenched with dew,
my hair with the dampness of the night."
I have taken off my robe —
must I put it on again?
I have washed my feet —
must I soil them again?
My lover thrusts his hand through the latch-opening;
my heart began to pound for him.

I rose to open for my lover,
and my hands dripped with myrrh,
my fingers with flowing myrrh,
on the handles of the lock.
I opened for my lover,
but my lover had left;
he was gone.
My heart sank at his departure.
I looked for him but did not find him.
I called for him but he did not answer.   *(5:2-6)*

Beloved:

Place me like a seal over your heart,
like a seal on your arm;
for love is as strong as death,
its jealousy unyielding as the grave.
It burns like a blazing fire,
like a mighty flame.
Many waters cannot quench love;
rivers cannot wash it away.
If one were to give all the wealth of his house for love,
it would be utterly scorned.   *(8:6-7)*

Lover:

You who dwell in the gardens with friends in attendance,
let me hear your voice!

Beloved:

Come away, my lover,
and be like the gazelle
or like a young stag
on the spice-laden mountains.   *(8:13-14, closing verses)*

133

Wedding

As usual, there has been considerable discussion regarding the origin of this work. An old tradition relates it to King Solomon (900 B.C.), whose name appears a couple of times in the text. Solomon was, after all, a poet and a prince who spoke much to the imagination. But the Song of Songs was not written by him. He was a man with a great many political marriages. I suspect it can only be the work of a woman.

Over the last hundred years it was generally assumed that this book was relatively young, originating around 300 B.C. A number of words supposedly point to this date. We are said undoubtedly to be dealing here with a group of wedding songs from Syria.

But use says very little about origin. It says a lot more about the experience of its users.

There apparently were in the north of Israel around 300 B.C. people who so clearly recognized true love in the words of the Song of Songs that they ritually consummated the marriage of the two lovers by means of it.

Is that not unbelievable? 300 B.C. During the consummation of the marriage. Senses, ego, and heart. Equal, mutual, dialogical. The other as such. The woman as initiative-taking, loving lover.

Monogamous. All or nothing. Radiating out toward full reality.

Such poetry conjures in me associations with the cover of this book: *The Kiss,* by Klimt; true love at its osmotic climax. "Thus may your love be, as that of these lovers. That is what we wish for you!"

It sounds like a blessing, and so it was. Toasts to their health by the wedding guests, promises and intentions of bride and groom.

Where has this deep insight, where has this love gone in the passing of the centuries? They can never really have been absent, in spite of all the Hellenistic dualism and all the misogyny. Common people have undoubtedly known of it deep in their hearts and have acted accordingly. It could not be any other way.

Grateful

The span of this poem was undoubtedly infinitely greater, deeper, and higher. Those who heard it — and later read it — understood that the love sung about here is something for which to be deeply *grateful.*

That is a feeling that we do not find with Eros and Narcissus. Eros w.d. is a hunter, be it courteous or discourteous. The eros of the philosophers climbs the ladder to heaven. Narcissus w.d. is at best a true consumer. Gratitude therefore is not in his vocabulary. But the love of Shulamite is so overwhelming that one does not know how to handle it and simply falls silent. "To what do I owe this part of my life?"

The believers of Israel had already given the answer before the question was posed. They thought that the question was improperly formulated. Not to *what,* but to *whom?* That can be none other than the Lord, the God of Abraham, Isaac, Jacob, and Moses, who, it is said, has given us life and freedom. This love is a fire from the Lord!

This understanding led to the rabbis' recognition of this poem as Holy Scripture, having arisen from the Holy One. To this very day, it has the authority of the holy, divine word for believing Jews and Christians, something which offers security and perspective for ordinary people in their daily lives. "Thus may you experience love together!"

But, alas, things went amiss with the processing of this Holy Scripture. The Song of Songs became spiritualized — to which it is admirably suited. It was viewed as an allegory that made clear something of the love that God gave to his people Israel and later, *mutatis mutandis,* of the love of God for the world. By means of this spiritualized, allegorical interpretation, human love can become a devotion not only restricted to one thing. It can now be extended to all of reality.

That is a decisive, liberating, perspective-creating extension. Its nucleus is wrapped up already in the Song of Songs. There all of reality shares in the joy of love. Paul and John later work this out in magisterial fashion.

The allegorical use of the love poetry of Shulamite, then, is not the problem: the devil sits in the exclusive spiritualization. The Song of Songs becomes a book for theologians. It is taken away from the common people. Shulamite is exiled to the Mount of the Sublime, which is inaccessible to common people. And so she is silenced. Up there, they of course have not a clue what to do with an initiative-taking shepherdess in love.

Ordinary and sacred love are divorced from each other for centuries. That could lead to no good. A dream image that cannot be applied to daily life is always a delusion. Holy love poetry that may not be consummated in reality leads to the absurd situation in which Eros w.d. and Narcissus w.d. determine what ordinary love is.

135

Herman, Will You Still Use Me?

The most explicit example of this that I can find is the story of the farmer's wife from Groningen, a northern Dutch province, who at night in bed, before going to sleep, would say to her husband: "Herman, will you still use me? Otherwise I shall turn to the Lord."

It is unbelievable and an outrage. From her words it is clear that we are dealing here with a Calvinist couple. Somewhere in their house sits the family Bible; perhaps they still read it regularly. The Song of Songs is, thus, within their reach. It even has for them divine authority. That the woman would say such a thing is, then, completely incomprehensible. But not unusual, not unusual!

I can get very depressed by such things. Is it any wonder that this woman's grandchildren no longer "turn to the Lord"?

Creativity

Hate bedevils and deforms. Love is creative[6] and reveals the true nature of things. Shulamite speaks words that seem strange to others. But people who know what love is recognize very well what she is trying to say about her beloved. They are simply convinced that she is talking about the wrong person.

Only Shulamite can look more deeply than Narcissus and also more deeply than the young man from *The Romance of the Rose*. They all look down to the bottom of the fountain. They have *experienced* the wonder and have made a *decision*. Therefore they are in the proper state for *beholding* and for *creativity*.

Suddenly that grubby shepherd is a king, a tree full of apricots in the middle of the meadow, a gazelle, a "young stag on spice-laden mountains." It had actually never occurred to him that way before.

She now knows him better than he will ever know himself and therefore she can help him come into his own right, so that he shines as

---

6. The term *creative* here is actually misplaced. Human love actually creates again, is *re-creative*, but the latter word is usually used in another sense.

the sun and beams like the moon. *If only they continue to love each other profoundly, osmotically,* with all that goes along with it, including mutuality and equality.

Thus functions love's creativity. That of *all* love, as well as love for other people in other we-circles, as well as love for animals, plants, and things.

Just in Love

"Shulamite and her shepherd boy are just in love," the superficial say. "They are still in seventh heaven and are too much in a tizzy to even know what to say. That will pass soon enough. Being in love soon disappears, love grows cold; then we'll wait and see whether they can hold on to each other."

"Just in love!" We have certainly heard enough of that sort of drivel, but it gives us an opportunity to finally say something about that important phenomenon of being *in love.*

On two previous occasions we have come up against this supposed "being in love": with Eros and with Narcissus. Let me give a quick summary.

Eros w.d. is not in love. He may call it that — no one can prevent him. But he is in no condition for true love, and therefore is not "in love" either. He has simply become fascinated by someone who belongs to his erotic type. This reflexively inflames his *desire* and he becomes excited. (Unless he is not after anything and knows himself a little.)

Just erotic fascination disappears and *just* sex grows cold. Then the attraction is gone and it is time to look around for someone else. Is this what the superficial have in mind?

Narcissus w.d. is not in love either. His longing is for a companion. He has not only become erotically fascinated, but has also been struck by the recognition of an image. This is a special experience, one that can really shake him up. When it is mutual, he can choose, and with or without so many words can form a companionship-pact for mutual benefit. Then he has a good partner, sometimes for life. But the first shock ebbs away. If the mutual benefit also ceases to exist . . .

Maybe this is what the superficial mean. But then they are forgetting something: *Narcissus w.d. has never really been in love.* He and Eros w.d.

belong to the type of person of whom La Rochefoucauld speaks when he says, "There are those who would never [talk about] be[ing] in love if they had not heard others speak of love."[7]

Being in love demands more than Eros w.d. and Narcissus w.d. together can muster. What, then?

I Repeat

There are a number of people who have never heard of the basic motivation of erotic fascination and of being struck by someone's appearance.

That is very misleading for some of them, since they insist that they are in love when they want to make love to someone or find their company pleasant. In two types of situations this can backfire.

The first is that of someone who is indeed in condition to love. She runs the risk of too quickly believing that she has found the right person and has the tendency to make hasty decisions that are later difficult to reverse.

Maybe she even lets it happen and later blames love.

"Yes, we were really in love then, yes we were!" No! They simply found each other nice and desirable.

It is also possible that she finds herself obliged time after time to break off the relationship. Then she can start to think that love is not for her. "What is wrong with me?" Probably nothing. Someone should tell her about the different types of human motivation.

A second type of situation in which a lack of this simple life experience can cause things to go wrong is that of lovers who find themselves in crisis. That does not mean that they do not love each other, but that something must happen in their relationship.

In the meantime, the two have become very sensitive, especially if they are unaware of the situation. If at this point one

---

7. "Il y a des gens qui n'auraient jamais été amoureux s'ils n'avaient entendu parler de l'amour." As quoted by J. H. van den Berg, *Het menselijk lichaam* [The human body] (Nijkerk, 1959).

of the two is fascinated, or even struck by someone else, then it is not impossible that he believes that he is in love and pursues it. The crisis then becomes irresolvable and the one in love feels justified in breaking it off. "It just happened!"

It is beyond the realm of life experience for such people that when it comes to love they never speak of experience alone, but also always of pursuing, of choices and decisions.

Such people, of course, are never really free of problems.

The Great Yearning

Shulamite is truly in love because she has access to her own heart. Therein lies the Great Yearning.

That is a notion that is older than our civilization. Plato already has his eros rising *to heaven,* moved by the Great Yearning. The agape of Shulamite, Paul, and John, on the other hand, falls like a gentle rain on a dry land *from heaven,* in order to fulfill the Great Yearning, to make it complete.

Those are words that I gladly use in this connection because they touch me: fulfillment, fullness. Full of happiness, peace, wholeness, righteousness. Truly present to the full reality, coming to full consciousness; two-handed. In love I already experience something of it with the beloved.

("Something? Something? No, everything!!!"

"No, the most beautiful part is yet to come."

"I can hardly imagine it. I do not need anything more beautiful and more exquisite than you."

"Nor do I. But it does not last forever, and not everyone is as happy as we are."

"That is true.")

Such words are not without risk. They may alienate those who would choose other words, even though they point to the same reality.

Love's Hope

Since Shulamite has access to her own heart, her senses and her ego can be tightly bound to it. Desires, longings, and yearnings can move in the same direction and be inspired by each other's ferment.

139

Then it can happen that when Shulamite meets someone, she is not only fascinated like Eros and struck like Narcissus, but she is also — if she remains open to it — *illuminated* by the Star of Hope.

It is hope that opens the heart.

"She is the one I have been looking for all my life! Could it really be true? If only it were, so that we could throw open the doors of the Garden of Gardens together! What do I owe this to? Now I see that I have been walking about in the dark. I have only just begun to live. Now everything is different. Yes, I am sure she is the one. But it is unbelievable, too good to be true. Could it actually be for me? What will I do if it is not so?"

The anxious questions are part of it, because the Star of Hope is covered by the clouds of fear from time to time.

Love's Hope is accompanied by a trance-like state. That is no wonder. (Or perhaps it is.) One's whole existence suddenly looks completely different. Before the Light shines, there is a certain dynamic balance between the person and the world; more with some than with others. There is a certain perspective on reality, knit together by experience, and the person thinks she knows more or less what can be expected from life. That may be a little, or that may be a lot. The Light of the Star always lets one see an astounding world, broader and more beautiful than we have ever dared to imagine in our wildest dreams.

The phenomenon can be compared to a religious experience. The one on whom it descends is disoriented for a while and not entirely accountable, complete with trembling hands and knocking knees. That trance-like state cannot be described with words. That is why approximately half of the world's literature and three-fourths of the songs are devoted to it. So I will not add another word.

Mutuality

Love's Hope is not love. Everything is still missing: mutuality, fire, and a decided turning. But what is not yet, yet can be. Can.

In order for *mutuality* to have its effect, the one in love sometimes has to do very little: simply make clear what her experiences are. Then there are suddenly two in the trance of hope (and fear) in love, and two people walk around with trembling hands and knocking knees.

"Could it be true? Yes, it is true! Us together! Really? Yes, really!"

There is something blessed about mutual hope in love. It is a fore-taste of the Kingdom of Heaven; a gift. But it is — forgive me — not yet Love.

People in love, who have been blinded by the Light of the Star, who are ignorant of this fact, get into trouble.

Choreography

Sometimes the person in love must do a *great* deal in order to effect the desired mutuality.

Maybe the other simply does not see her, no matter what she says and does. Then it is to be hoped that he does not just pretend that he is also in love — just to play some kind of mean power game, or in order to stroke his ego. Then he has the power to choreograph the life of the person in love; a cruel pas de deux, with complicated moves of attraction and rebuff. It can last for months, or even years. But the ending had already been written long before: she remains behind, alone and hopeless, on an empty stage.

In the last few years an alternative ending has been written, thanks to the women's movement: with an elegant Judo move she tosses him off stage and receives the applause of the relieved public.

Sometimes a little theater does no harm. There are always those lovers who have perfected their "in love" routine in order to land attractive bodies in bed or to gain other advantages (money, prestige, leisure). From the fairy tales we know that they can quickly be unmasked with three simple tests (two is too few; four is too many).

Love's Hope that ends up with nothing because the candi-date wants nothing to do with it always remains with a person. Sometimes in the form of irritating complexes, if some such nauseating game is played. (The Star of Hope was an illusion. Next time I will look more closely. That will never happen to me again. All men are beasts, all women are whores, etc.)

But fortunately sometimes hope in love can also stay with

a person as a fond memory, on which one looks back with joy. "So, it really does exist!"

That is also the great benefit of puppy love: they can get a taste of it.

Love's Fire

The Light of the Star is necessary for Love's Hope, but is not sufficient for true love.

True love requires a spark to get the *fire* going. "The fire of the Lord," Shulamite says.

There are not many today who are willing simply to repeat after her that the spark comes from the Lord — if indeed they still believe in the necessity of the fire, no matter from whom or from where it is to be expected.

Because where there is no fire, there is no love. And where the fire is not continually provided with more fuel, the fire dies. What remains are only ashes and coals. That must be avoided at all costs — or at least almost all costs.

That is what the last chapter of this book is about, but it is also good to clarify right now that no one but the lovers can throw more fuel on the fire.

If the spark jumps, one must wait, but not passively. The spark jumps — or fails to jump — only when lovers *intensively interact with one another;* make a fixed investment in each other — in hope of blessing.

Entrusting

In (intensive) loving interaction with each other, it readily becomes apparent whether or not lovers can confidently *entrust themselves to one another.*

Entrust. That is one of my last key words in dealing with love. Not only is it related to "trust," "trustworthy," and "betroth," but also to "true." Way in the background stands the Indo-European *dreu,* which means both "oak" and "absolute certainty."

One of the essential conditions for love is that I am offered the absolute certainty that I need not be on my guard. I can expose myself with complete trust, because the intimate things I have entrusted remain "between us." It can therefore never be used against me. That is also true of the Great Yearning: vulnerability is permissible, to be able to fully entrust oneself, to lay down the armor. Without risk. "I'm gonna lay down my sword and shield, down by the riverside." (It is possible to entrust oneself in varying degrees. One entrusts other, less intimate thoughts to an acquaintance than those one entrusts to a good friend. We will return to this in depth in the next chapter.)

To the one, true, great love one must be able to entrust *everything*, in *the unassailable certainty* that it will remain between them.

Osmosis Again

Lovers come to know each other inside and out. This can be abused. Those who have an affair are continually trying to justify themselves by disparaging the one to whom they are being unfaithful. But that is something that is even more intolerable. Love, at its climax, has a double osmotic effect, biochemically and Shulamithically.

When making love, the lovers absorb through the skin the temperaments, the body fluids of each other. Very personal, strictly unique, biochemical mixtures and bonds, which is why people have rightly always dealt very circumspectly with strangers.

The bodies of people who have made love are osmotically *changed in terms of their biochemical composition.* They have taken up into themselves something very intimate of the other.

Those who make love to someone else while the biochemistry of the other is still in their temperaments are biochemically unfaithful. They do not keep "between us" that which has been entrusted to them in complete confidence. That is why it is necessary to have the absolute confidence that this will never happen.

How can one completely erotically entrust oneself to a lover when one is not absolutely certain that his lover's body does not contain the temperaments of a stranger?

But there is also a Shulamithic side to osmosis, which is

perhaps the true side. It is not without reason that ancient wisdom thought that temperaments and breathing had to do with heart and soul. How that connection was made is unclear, but it is more than simply metaphorical or analogical.

During the climax of loving intercourse — both inside and outside the bedroom — something of the intimate self penetrates the skin, which acts as meeting point, from the one lover to the other. And so they each remain the same, while at the same time absorbing something into themselves of the Shulamithic intimacy.

"I've got you under my skin," Nat King Cole sang. His lover finds it wonderful, but only if there is absolute certainty that the intimacy that he has from her under his skin will never end up with a stranger.

That is why it is advisable after the death of a lover not to start something new too quickly or too easily. One still possesses too much of the biochemical and Shulamithic intimacy of the lost lover in oneself. The grieving process serves, among other things, to make part (or all) of the beloved's biochemistry one's own, and/or to cleanse oneself by ridding oneself of part (or all) of it.

It occurs to me that during the sexual revolution we did not fully grasp the importance of these osmotic aspects of promiscuity. Perhaps, in the heat of the battle, that was impossible. But in the meantime we have all learned something. I can no longer comprehend that there are still people who do not have the least problem with promiscuity. I suppose that they are simply completely at the mercy of vegetative pressures, desperate from loneliness, or misled by the worn-out slogan that everyone must reflexively do whatever turns them on.

If, during the intensive interaction of two people in love, the Light of the Star of Hope does not quickly shine in the Fire, through the experience of unassailable certainty that they can completely entrust themselves to each other, there is no future in it.

Too bad, terrible, awful. Perhaps one should grieve, or more than that. To finally stand before the door of the Garden of Gardens and then to have to turn back. Could anything be worse?

But, oh daughters of Jerusalem, to be half wrong is better than to be completely complacent. Do not think, "O well, everyone has moments like this. I am not going to complain. I will get used to it. Things like this must grow." Remember the Song of Songs: "I charge you by the gazelles, and by the does of the field: Do not arouse or awaken love until it so desires."

A love pact that is drawn up on the basis of (mutual) hope in love alone is defective. If the experience of unassailable certainty is present, Love's Hope has become Love's Fire. That is the "in love" of Shulamite and her shepherd. The "in love" of certainty and expectation.

It is great enough to take a chance on. *Strong enough to last a lifetime.* As long as the Fire is kept burning. We will come back to that. There is still another "as long as. . . ."

Decided Turning

Eros *must know what he is doing* when he acts on his reflexive fascination. Narcissus is still not finished; he must *choose.* That is an act of will, a question of honestly weighing pros and cons. For this he needs freedom and responsibility and the courage to give his life some kind of shape. Some, however, do not dare or are unable to make the choice.

Lovers must Shulamithically make that choice by passing through a *crucial point of decision.* They must devote themselves to each other by engaging their entire self-consciousness, and thus create a whole new reality for themselves. Only herein does love have that wonderful creativity. "You are the most beautiful, the best, the loveliest. You are everything to me, the most central meaning, the deepest experience." *And that is unassailable certainty.*

That is an essential condition for two people who want to love each other and want to *remain* ardently in love.

Inside and Out

Lovers decidedly devote themselves to each other and thereby exclude all others as *lovers.*
Not as loved ones, not as friends, not as neighbors. As such they are included.

145

But as lovers they are excluded, because only the one can be that, on the basis of a decision that has creatively altered reality.

Like a Rush

"I never knew that love was so complicated," Frank says with a smile. "Eros, Narcissus, Shulamite (never heard of her), and two kinds of being in love. It is not that way at all. With me and Darla it was just all of a sudden, like a rush. It was great!"

"And so it should be," was my reply. "In everyday life, lovers are happy, contented, and at peace. Then it does not have to have a name. What is more, a book like this is then simply confusing, since it can cause a loss of openness. But I see around me that love is often not esteemed highly enough. My attempt at restoration forces me to be somewhat complicated. It is like one of those old windup alarm clocks. As long as it was running you never gave the thing a second glance. But when it broke down, you pulled the thing apart only to be surprised at how many parts there were and how intricately the thing was put together."

"But when those new electronic things stop working you just throw them away, because it is cheaper to replace it than it is to repair it," Frank replied.

Mine was not a very good analogy, I guess.

Everything but the Decision

"It is important to me that you recognize yourself in what I have written," I said.

He was quiet for a time. Then he nodded somewhat reluctantly.

"Yes. In *everything but the decision*. I have never made the decision, at least not in the deeply penetrating way that you describe. I have always assumed that love is just something that happens to you; not something that you also make yourself."

"I was afraid of that," I said, "because you said: 'That *was*

146

great.' Past tense. Were you not able to decidedly turn yourself? Did you not want to?"

The answer came three weeks later by telephone.

"I did not want to. I did not want to go that far. I had to leave an escape route open."

"And what about Darla?"

"Yes, Darla. I was not fair to her. I see now that I was playing with fire all those years. She deserves the credit for the fact that it has turned out all right. I sometimes walked mighty close to the edge, and to tell the truth, I have even almost fallen in a few times. But she always knew how to grab me just before I dropped."

"Today," I said patriarchally. "Today if you hear his voice." He laughed.

"It already happened. Do you think I would have called you if it hadn't? We have an extremely emotional week behind us; but I won't bore you with the details.

"What I did want to ask you is whether such a belated decision has *retroactive force*. Darla says it does, but I am not so sure."

"Yup, you two were like children, crazy about each other, playing hide-and-go-seek among the stars . . ."

"Okay, enough, enough. I already know. Then everything is all right."

In a certain sense such a crucial point of decision can be compared with what in religion is known as a conversion. That is also a decided turning that excludes all other gods on the basis of something that is experienced as a gift. A conversion is also the giving of an irrevocable turn to life. It is like a knot in one's (experiential) timeline.

I was unable to express myself in other than sublime, nearly sacred terms. Perhaps that suggests that a love pact sealed in this way can no longer be undone.

Unfortunately, that is not the case. The cracks do not form part of the pattern, but they are still there. All lovers will lose each other. Some to death, others to nonlife. Love is for that reason something that must be handled with extreme care.

Walter Again

He was the one who wondered why you would keep a cow when you could get milk from so many sources. Moreover, he could not imagine what a book on love could possibly contain, other than a list of useful lines for picking up women. Finally he advised me not even to start, because "writing about love evokes hate."

The man — in his late thirties — is not stupid, not uncivilized, and is fairly easy to get along with. I would not want to deny him a certain depth either.

And yet he speaks in the fashion of a cynical Narcissus who cannot even find the way to his own heart. *Dressaten?* A one-armed, technical upbringing? He does not let on.

He also eagerly reads the proofs of the chapter on Shulamite. That is very important to me, because I wrote it, among other reasons, in order to communicate with him. His commentary is very disappointing, though. He labels me an incorrigible, old-fashioned romantic and thinks that we live in a new era of which I understand nothing, no matter how you look at it.

Then he says something that makes me wonder whether I have not perhaps completely failed: "You cannot begin to hate all the rest of them because of one person."

Hate? Hate? What I am trying to get across is just the opposite: that *you can love all of reality precisely because of that one person.* That one is the Great Lover, who lets me come into my own right and sets me free, so that I can love myself and so that everyone and everything can participate in love in their own way.

What am I supposed to do with Walter? The gap of the mutual lack of comprehension seems unbridgeable.

No Lover

All this writing and (re)reading sometimes creates a feeling of uneasiness in me. There are countless people who yearn for a lover, but cannot find one. What are they supposed to do with all my high-sounding statements? Are they not extremely uncompassionate? Are they not just easy expressions made from an ivory tower by a man who has never lacked anything in love? Take, for example, the statement that "you can love all of reality precisely because of that one person."

And if that one person is not there in your life and never has been, even though you have desperately yearned for one? *Does that mean you cannot love all of reality?*

You can, but it is a very difficult battle, one which not everyone wins. To yearn for a lover but not to find one is a kind of suffering from "lack of fulfillment," a suffering from the cracks in the mosaic of existence. True love with a lover is not for everyone who yearns for it. We see it all around us. It is not very pleasing. We must recognize that fact, even though we do not want to accept it.

When viewed from this perspective, such suffering demands an answer. But what answer?

Revolution is in my opinion the best answer to begin with. True revolution does not simply put up with the cracks but tries to do something about them. It attempts to take its destiny into its own hands, and no difficulty is too great.

"Is there something wrong with me? Just tell me, please, then I will do something about it, with or without help. If I cannot find my type where I am, then I will go elsewhere. Over and over again, trying, investing, dreaming, and if need be, playing along. Disappointed? Then I'll try again, because it will not be the case that I do not find true love. I will fight for it in order to remain true to myself, and I will never settle for less."

What lies behind this admirable answer is, in addition to a large dose of determination and ego-love, mostly *hope.* And it is the hope that opens and makes accessible the heart, where the Great Yearning is concealed, so that it can be decidedly turned. Hope always works in opposition to the defensive reactions.

Those who are rebellious in this way can love all of reality. Hope creates life, and therefore love.

But how does one arrive at hope if one is not illumined by the Star that shines for lovers alone? Let's leave that question for the time being.

Grief is, as far as I am concerned, the next best answer to a lack of a lover; just honest grief.

"I am apparently no one's type. Never in my life has anyone spent more than five minutes considering me as a potential lover. No one sees anything in me, no matter what I do, and no matter what advice I follow. Sex is the only thing possible; and even that hardly ever. True love is not for me. What am I supposed to do?"

Those who are forced by circumstances to speak in such a heart-rending manner go in a couple of different directions with their answer. The direction of bitterness is the most dangerous. Hope is surrendered and the way to the heart is closed with the protective plug of bitterness and hate as a means of self-preservation. This plug, moreover, has the tendency to spread like a cancerous tumor. *Before one knows it, one has become a bitter person, instead of a person with just one bitter plug.* The pain of failure is thus overcome, because a bitter person cannot be hurt. But at what price? All love has become impossible.

The direction of grief is best — for those who are strong enough and can count on the necessary support. Those who grieve recognize the awful facts, but do not accept them. Nevertheless, they no longer make the effort to change them. (Perhaps that is too hasty; that is not generally the case.)

But those who grieve do not close up their hearts with a plug. They do not give up hope, but maintain the possibility of loving someone. They can turn to someone or something with the offer of love A, B, or C, and then their lives gain a new perspective. The joy that that gives can soften the pain to the point where it is bearable. For grief and joy are not mutually exclusive. It is possible to experience grief over one thing while rejoicing over another.

But the vulnerability remains. At the most inopportune and unforeseen moments, the pain of the failure to find one's own authentic, unique, true love appears again. That can happen with the simple sight of a couple walking down the street holding hands. It can happen while watching television, while reading a book, or at a party that one attends alone. "One hundred times it comes off without a hitch and now suddenly everything falls apart again, damn it. Will I never get used to it?"

No. Those who choose grief never really get used to it.

Now they must again begin the difficult struggle not to give up hope. Elsewhere I have called that "the labyrinth of pain."

"Suddenly nothing has changed; such is life."

"Indeed, such is life, but we do not just have to lie down and take it."

150

"Easy for you to talk."

That is true.

There are in addition to these many other in-between forms, and the answer never need be definitive.

Perhaps on Vacation

It was years ago already. She was at that time over forty and had always been alone. For a long time she had continued to hope and dream that he — the man of her dreams — would some day find her.

She knew life well enough to know that she should actually actively look for him, but she found that to be indecorous. Women should wait, she opined, and her friends agreed with her.

She knew the Song of Songs well enough, but she did not dare identify herself with Shulamite on any of those points. Women must not take the initiative, everyone in her circle thought.

Her hope had become but a small, flickering light. "He is not going to find me; perhaps he does not even exist, but . . . ."

Every spring that changed. She and her friends made plans for a long vacation, far beyond the horizons of her everyday — and rather boring — existence.

Then she dreamed that on board the ship, or during the intermission at the concert, she would be addressed by him. He would say that from the first moment he saw her. . . . Each year she would imagine what would happen.

A couple of times it even seemed like it might be the time, she thought, but her friends noticed and broke the man down into pieces on the ground, with their sour, sneering comments about his appearance or mannerisms.

And so she had a boring life, interspersed with spoiled vacations.

He did not find her. To her grief. But hope was never completely extinguished. She was not bitter, and therefore could continue to love.

151

The question as to how a person arrives at that hope has now become even more pressing.

Hope Is a Light

The hope that we have in mind here is the *light* that puts a person in a position to continue to hope that the Great Yearning will some day be fulfilled and that therefore love is possible and necessary. Sometimes that is expectation against all odds, when all the observable facts point in the opposite direction.

Since we have all experienced that there is such a thing as vain hope, hope always goes together with fear. That is even the case with Love's Hope. Then the fulfillment appears so close to being within our grasp that it turns one completely upside-down. "Could it really be true?"

How does one arrive at such hope if the beloved is not there (anymore) or never was? That was the question of the preceding paragraph.

The answer is that the beloved always — or almost always — has been there, in a certain manner of speaking. Most people are brought up in love. Those who brought them up taught them what love is. They were examples of what lovers are for their children and sketched the first lines of their dream image. They caressed their senses, established their egos, and caused their hearts to rejoice. Thus the children were introduced to the mystery of the true nature of reality. In this way they came to self-consciousness. (The love of those who bring up children points away from itself. The fact that the growing children must detach themselves from those who bring them up in order to continue to grow and to be able to turn back to them does not diminish this in any way.)

Almost everyone has, via her upbringing, a reservoir of positive experiences, in which a glimmer is preserved of a shining future. That reservoir functions like a sort of battery in happy children that can later let the light of hope shine. In the common, everyday, good life of a child, that battery is regularly charged by the loving interaction with full reality. There are people who can last a lifetime with such a childhood battery, but most people cannot. In many lives the battery runs dead, through short circuits or just plain use. Then the Light of Hope goes out. Unless . . .

The second answer is that the Light of Hope continues to shine for

152

those without lovers if they *believe* in the future: if they maintain a positive outlook on the future.

Both the capitalist and Marxist forms of the materialistic hope for the future have lost their credibility. The Marxist obviously so. The capitalist continues to hold out in those regions where people generally live under the motto, "We will not end up the same way; we will think of something."

One can be satisfied with this kind of consumerism, which reminds us of Narcissus w.d. Those who are unable or unwilling to do so and yet do not want to give up hope and want to continue to love are referred to another belief,[8] albeit not religious. That is not surprising, because according to ancient wisdom, *"now there remain these three: faith, hope and love, but the greatest is love."* [9]

Just Her Love

Whom does she love, this Shulamite?

That seems to be a good question. But the answer is right before us: the shepherd, of course. Who else?

That is my answer too, but there are differences of opinion. We will not rehearse here the discussion that goes along with them in order not to get lost in tangentials. Yet it is good to say something about it.

The first alternative opinion is that she is in fact in love with *herself*. I reject that. Love is not a means, but an end. For Shulamite, it is a question of the other, the other as such. Even Eros and Narcissus cannot get along without the other. They exist because they are other. That seems essential to me. That is why the Phoenix is relegated to the stage and subsequently the ontic experience is measured out so broadly. Shulamite needs her ego-love in order to reach her heart. This is essentially different than the love she has for her man.

A second opinion that I reject is that in the shepherd, she loves Love.

8. In fact, I have exchanged the question, "How does one arrive at hope?" for another question: "How does a person arrive at hope in the future?" My (hopefully discerning) answer is found in my *Christelijke geloofsopvoeding* [Nurturing Christian faith] (Kampen, 1991).

9. I Cor. 13. See also *Geliefde gedichten* (Beloved poems), collected by Wim Zaal (Amsterdam, 1972).

The man is, in this view, also a means, but now in order to achieve something better. Here we meet the eros of Plato again, sometimes in a baptized version. People who think thus say, "Shulamite does not really love that man; she really loves God, maybe without even realizing it. We must tell her. She is better off jumping right over the man — with his foul, lustful, erotic desire — and loving God directly and therefore celibately. That is what the Holy Virgin did."

This disparaging of the sovereign realms of the senses and the ego goes directly contrary to my deepest convictions. *If agape is exclusively spiritualized, women are surrendered in daily life to wolves and egoists and patronized by vermin who consider themselves sublime.* Women no longer accept that. As a result, however, we find those confusing, actually superfluous struggles between men and women, who, if they would love correctly, would together form the true image of God, who is Love. Those are mysterious words, which are probably difficult to understand, but I have no others to express my indignation at this moment. (And I do not mean to say anything negative about true love between persons of the same gender.)

Thanks to agape, Shulamite can love her shepherd as her only true lover. She can, thanks to that same agape, love God as her only true God. And she can, in her own way, also love others, animals, plants, things, the wind, the earth, the water, fire. She can love all of reality thanks to agape: the other, the Other, others, and other things.

And she does, if I have listened to her carefully.

But she holds a burning love for that man as the loving lover, as such. Not for the sake of something above, beyond, or behind him, nor for lack of anything better. He is just her love, and she his.

9. We-Circles

Interaction

Love is put into practice in our everyday interaction. That alone keeps the Fire burning and the covenant intact. Nothing else can. Those who experience inexplicable difficulties in love must engrave this on their minds.

This loving interaction has until now remained more or less beyond the spotlight of our attention. It came into view once or twice, for example, in the transition from Love's Hope to Love's Fire. "The spark jumps — or fails to jump — only when lovers intensively interact with one another." Then it becomes evident whether they can really completely *entrust* themselves to each other.

The rest of this book is devoted to the interaction of lovers with each other (and with all of reality).

As a result of the currents of the last forty years, self-evident, assumed, generally accepted patterns of loving interaction are disappearing with stunning rapidity, or have already disappeared. In part that is to our advantage, since they undoubtedly were no longer adequate. But in another (small) part, essential and useful patterns were simply swept away by the current, leaving confusion everywhere. Completely normal chaos, according to the Beck sisters.

Therefore we will try to bring to light something that might help (for the time being) to find new, useful forms of interaction.

Limited

"All of reality participates in love," we have discovered. Because I am other, I can love; reality is suited to love. Thanks to agape I can devote myself to all of reality with my senses, ego, and heart in order to make a covenant of love, so that the true nature of things can come to light and so that I can experience something of the fullness toward which the Great Yearning inclines.

These sublime, mystical-sounding words are all very, very true, but there is also something else that must be noted: human capacity for loving interaction with reality is *limited* in time, space, and action. We are not God: eternal, omnipresent, and infinite in love.

Moreover—let it be emphatically noted—human energy is limited. (I prefer to use H. L. Bergson's term *élan vital* here, since it points to the power of life of the whole human person.) The arrogant cry, "Anything goes!" is already on the way to silence. We have been made wise by shame and harm, with the exception of a small group of people who always lag behind.

Those who want to be infinite in love run the risk of never loving anyone or anything again, or worse: to begin to feel much contempt for many and finally to begin to hate. Or they are forced by lack of élan vital to leave behind everyday interaction—where everything comes down to earth—and retire to the Mount of the Sublime. Then they can sit and meditate, smiling contentedly, among the statues of saints who stare at the sun, and hermits who stare at their navels. Very imposing, but not very effective. Such a love is of no use for anyone or anything.

Or they are strangled by the chords of quick, fleeting, and one-sided attempts at unlimited loving interaction. Then they let no one and nothing come into its own right, least of all themselves. The result is usually that same withdrawal from everyday things: dead tired, disappointed, lonely, and abandoned. In love, there is much that is not good, but the good is much. What we should be talking about is not *all* of reality, but rather *full* reality. A week has but 168 hours. Neither my arms nor my self-consciousness can embrace everything.

But they can embrace something. Something of the fullness. *Pars pro toto.* In the part I love the whole.

Circles

If we limit ourselves for the time being to love for the other, then we can say that a person can make a number of different types of love covenants, which lie in concentric circles around her. I call them "we-circles"; the "we" excludes the bondedness. A we-circle includes the people with whom the individual, the "person," has more or less the same type of covenant, and the same degree of entrustedness, and the same degree of intimacy.

Whether the people who are included also belong to each other's we-circles is not important, although socially it is important. A community is — among other things — a group of people who belong to each other's we-circle.

Interaction in each we-circle — call them A, B, C, and D — is different, where the investment of élan vital may be expressed in terms of *time* (duration and frequency), *place*, and *action* (nature and depth). In other words, in every we-circle it is a question of *what* people do with each other and *how* deeply; *where* they do it and *when*; *how long*, and *how frequently*.

The next chapter deals with this under "basic forms."

Everything, Always, Everywhere, Deeply

With lovers there is always the healthy but unrealistic desire to do everything, always, everywhere, deeply together, without others along. It is precisely one of the distinguishing characteristics of the Fire in love.

Over time it becomes impossible, because even lovers do not live on an uninhabited island, in a tent above the tree line, or in a cottage in the meadow. And even then they would have to make a division of tasks in order to allow the reality around them to come into its own right, because the one can do it better than the other.

But from time to time it must be so: just the two of them, doing everything, always, everywhere, deeply together, day and night. Completely invested in each other.

That is one of the ways to let the Fire flare up again.

To the degree that the circle lies farther from the center, the investment diminishes and the number of people who can be included in the circle increases (people who are nothing more than acquaintances, who see each other perhaps once a month, here and there, and do just a couple of things together, like drink coffee or just chat.)

It is striking how frequently difficulties are caused in love by a lack of insight into the structure of we-circles and by an absolutely inefficient distribution of investments.

To this can be added that a great deal of élan vital must be invested in other activities (work, education, sport, politics, social obligations). What is expended there cannot be applied to love. The result is easy to guess: the Fire of Love is in danger of being extinguished and the covenant becomes frayed. That is generally superfluous, however, for those who love each other in the manner of Shulamite.

The Double Center

"Here I am" — and then I point to my heart — "the middle, the center of the world of my we-circles. But since my beloved entered my life, it has become a *double center*. My beloved is the most central meaning of my world of meaning and my interaction with her incites the deepest experiences in my world of experience."

The double center, the "we" of the lovers is the true fixed center. That is the nucleus. Around it are bunched the other circles of entrustedness; the we-circles. Those of beloved ones, friends, acquaintances, names, faces, passersby, and so on to the ends of the earth. They are for the time being just words. What they might contain remains to be seen.

It is good here to give the emphatic reminder that the "we" of two lovers cannot be some sort of symbiotic unit, wherein the two people lose their "being other" because they are taken up into each other, possess each other, are fused to one another, or the like. Instead, the "we" of lovers is a dialogical relationship. If that is not the case, everything ends. For the double center, it is absolutely essential that there be two people, equal and free. The osmotic character of love does not bring to an end the "being other" of the two, but is a result of it. Those who do not see this run the great risk of neglecting the beloved in the loving interaction where investment of time, place, and action are concerned.

The beloved is our closest neighbor and therefore our first responsibility. Not the only responsibility, but the first. If we should unexpectedly be forced to choose, if it should come to that, then we have already creatively passed the point of the decision of Shulamite. "You are the one."

Moreover, what does it profit a man if he gains the whole world but loses his Lover, at which his soul experiences unspeakable suffering? And that is guaranteed to happen if he does not make sufficient investment in the loving interaction of the double center.

The investment has a centripetal effect (inward, toward the double center). This is more important now than ever, since in these times there are a number of forces that are working in the opposite direction: centrifugally.

You Have Been Given to Me, I Found You, but I Must Keep Seeking You

Consider, for example, a normal, everyday couple, Fritz and Annie. No (really distressing) defensive reactions, no inaccessible hearts. From all appearances, they are each other's type, having chosen each other, creatively and decidedly turned toward each other. And all that without ever giving it a name, very open and natural.

Could you ask for anything more? Yes — the proper rigging.

After five years of marriage and two healthy, lovely children, they took over Father's business. They had a very special meaning in the family, both the business and Father.

The business was not just a source of income, and Father was not just a family member. Both were viewed with a sort of religious aura. The business was inhabited by a strong, demanding deity of which Father was prophet and high priest.

They had always chuckled about it, but it never really bothered them because it was a good business and Father was a good man.

But the man continued to follow them and the business took over and *everything was made subordinate to it.* Fritz became the sublime businessman mentioned above, who is willing to offer love on the altar of Higher Interests.

Their love was no longer the double center of their world. The business had become that. It was their only subject of conversation, because for the time being the children were no problem. It was their common concern when things (seldom) threatened to go awry.

It was their common, positive experience when it was successful (usually). Their lives were dedicated to something higher than their love: the business!

Until Annie had to cut herself loose, because the business became too complicated through all the mergers and new incorporations. Moreover, the children began to have problems at school.

Suddenly she discovered — all alone, in her little house — that in the last few years they had never had anything together except that goddamn stinking business.

When she explained that to Fritz, he could not understand what she was saying. There were scenes and fights. She began to "lead her own life." And that was just fine with him. Until a year later he found out via a friend in the business that she had a friend on the side.

"Unfaithful!" he said to me indignantly. "Who would ever have expected that of Annie?"

There is no talking to him.

I try to explain to him that faithfulness in love consists of everyday loving interaction, of bringing fuel for the fire.

No connection. For him, a lover means *having* someone. You are each other's inalienable *possession*. Only with such support behind us can we dedicate ourselves to our obligations in society and the church. And for Fritz that consists first of the business, then the local Chamber of Commerce, nine commissions, four assemblies, and a bunch of executive something or others ... he lost count. In any case, they were all tasks that he simply could not ignore. *Love was always for him what was left when he closed the books.* Another, new central meaning had arisen in his life, and his deepest experiences no longer related to his lover, but to the business.

And so they lost each other, and now he feels aggrieved.

"You have been given to me, I found you, but I must continue to seek you," I say to him. "That's the way love is."

160

He gives me a puzzled look. "You have to be unassailably certain about your wife. Unassailably certain that she too finds the gift of love the most important task in life."

"And how was I supposed to do that with the business?"

"You would have figured it out, perhaps in some other way, or perhaps without it. I don't know. Anyone who finds a business, any business, more important than his beloved enters a path that leads away from her."

"Irresponsible drivel! That is not the last word on this matter."

"No, I promise you that."

"My mother and her mother would never have done such a thing."

"They are different."

He nods bitterly.

"I am just beginning to understand that."

External Centers

In the foregoing case there are three important points.

First, Annie and Fritz exchanged the double center of their love for the business. It began to function as an *external center* in their marriage. As long as it lasted it seemed like a great means of communication, but it began to work centrifugally when Annie had to break away. They fell out of the habit of being lovers, because for so much time they were only indirectly interacting with each other, except for a bit of erotica.

We see similar problems with an external center in couples who invest everything in their children and hardly anything in each other. When the empty nest comes along, they also seem alienated from each other.

There are countless other examples. I will just mention that the long, drawn-out process of building a house can have the same effect. When the house is ready, the love is gone. I personally know a couple that saw the problem coming and quickly exchanged the new house for another run-down place that needed to be fixed up. At least that way they still had something together.

And yet it must be admitted that some couples last a lifetime with just such an external center. In these times, where everything changes so

161

rapidly, it is very risky to put all the eggs in this one basket. (It is possible to *overtax* a relationship for a time, for example, while one of the lovers pursues studies or achieves some other external goal. But that must always be done with eyes wide open, fully aware of the risks, and for a limited time. What is borrowed from the double center must later be paid back.)

The second point in Fritz and Annie's case is Fritz's idea that lovers possess one another. Usually, in practice, that means that the man possesses the woman. How does a nice, modern man fall into such worn ruts? He is no oceanic coalescence. But neither is he married, that I know for sure.

Both he and Annie failed to understand that although they first took over the business, it was not long before the business took over them. They were no longer lovers with a business, but business people with a lover in the few spare moments they had.

That cannot help but go awry. Annie understood that. Fritz did not; he wanted to remain a businessman with a lover.

In order to justify his own unfaithfulness, he later came up with this idea of possessing each other. *He just invented a theory that would not make him look too bad.* That is the pitfall of all theorists, great and small.

Third, Fritz states that his mother and mother-in-law would never have acted this way. They were different people, I said. Is that true?

Marriage

What precisely has caused the remarkable chaos in the West that Beck and Beck-Gernsheim find so "completely normal"? It is almost as though millions of *marriages* broke down on cue in the Western world. What has changed? What are the centrifugal forces?

Fritz is far and away no exception, and the appeal he makes to his mother and mother-in-law is not completely off the wall. Before we closely examine the changes through the ideas of Beck and Beck-Gernsheim, we must also point out that *we are running the risk of unintentionally changing the subject.*

Up to this point, we have talked about love, not marriage. These two terms for a long time now have not referred to the same reality. The span of love is greater than that of "love for and with the Lover." This book deals in particular with that latter covenant, but we apparently cannot avoid saying something about the broader span as well.

Moreover, what has been said about love is just as valid for those who are not (yet) able to marry because they are of the same gender. There are also those marriages formed with a goal other than the public formation and confirmation of love. Finally, there are also, alongside traditional marriages, all kinds of love covenants in which love is formed and confirmed.

And yet the pressing question remains, why do so many marriages (and other love covenants) fall apart? Is it inevitable? Completely normal? Then it is advisable not even to start (again), or to do it in such a way that an easy escape route remains open.

My own answer — which I will further explain below — is short and clear: the chaos is normal since we live in a time of transition, in which all kinds of centrifugal forces are at work. But that is in and of itself no loss, and the worst confusion is already behind us. For people who love each other, *the future is brighter than ever.*

Individualism-Personalism

In the West, so-called individualism has gained momentum over the last thirty years. There are a number of collaborating factors in this, such as increases in buying power, free time, education, training, and information. There is also the change of the nature of authority, the moral failure of absolute power, the explosive increase in mobility, and the loss of social controls.

Whoever reviews these — in part related, in part overlapping — factors will note that the possibility for individualization differs from (sub)culture to (sub)culture. There has always been individualism, but much less so than today. *It is a luxury that usually only persons who possess a certain degree of independence — not only creative-intellectual, but also socioeconomic — can afford.* They have the room to give shape to their own lives.

An Aside

The luxury of individualism was, at the end of the eighteenth century in Europe, reserved for (primarily male) members of the aristocratic and patrician classes. Rousseau was the one who put the new ideals for raising children into words. What he noted in regard to *customs* is very important in this regard.

"Emile," his (male) charge, was permitted to have but *one* habit: that he have *no* habits. He was required always to choose and decide.

It would be two centuries before these and other ideas of Rousseau would be picked up again by members of a completely different social strata. First by men, but then later, suddenly, to a much greater extent by women.

In traditional (sub)cultures, it is normal that one fits oneself (some-what) into the established patterns. That provides a great deal of security. It keeps the whole in existence and the individual knows what his place is. He does not have to choose continuously and thus is not required to carry on endless, time-consuming, faction-creating negotiations. "Custom is the flywheel of conduct!" Thorndike said at the beginning of this century.

In other words, until recently, it was also the case in the West that people conformed to the established forms — ecclesiastical, professional, social, etc. — of the society of which they were a part. Who would marry whom, for example, was not entirely predetermined, but in closed societies that was indeed the case, at least in broad outline. Suitors from other (sub)cultures were forcefully rejected and one kept a careful eye on one's own daughters, because they had been set aside for certain young men from the same (sub)culture. The few who had objections to such arrangements quickly came into conflict with their society, especially with those who had authority in such matters (cf. the story of the patriarch).

Sometimes it worked, sometimes it did not. That has given us some wonderful love stories that once and a while ended in tragedy, such as Romeo and Juliet.

I therefore define individualists as independent people who are not prepared simply to comply with the expectations of their society.

Another Aside

The word "individualism" is rather confusing in this connection, but because it is generally used, I will conform (!) to common

164

usage. I would prefer the term "personalism," because it better indicates that we are dealing with a question of *freedom and responsibility*. Moreover, this word has no disturbing secondary meanings.

For example, in using the term "individual" I do not have in mind its oldest sense (= indivisible), but rather the type of person that thinks that he cannot afford to allow himself to care about anyone else. This is someone like Vincent, who cannot love anyone because he is self-sufficient.

Furthermore, Narcissus w.d. is also in the habit of calling himself an individualist when in fact he is nothing more than a superficial consumer.

Another disturbing sense is that of the compulsive trouble-maker, who lives in discord with everyone and everything and who does *not* do what society expects of him, without reflection or choice. For me the individual is the human person, in all his or her worth.

Individualists are, therefore, not "conformers," but "choosers" and "deciders." They are not automatically "part of" a society, but they usually "go along with" society. But if the choice is more or less forced upon them, they disappear again as soon as they get the chance.

"I'm Annie!"

I do not know Fritz's mother very well, but I do know Annie's mother quite well. She sat next to me in school, from kindergarten until what we then called the sixth class of elementary school.

Her name is Janna Essink and she is the oldest daughter of a farmer from the Dutch province of Drenthe. Her mother and grandmothers all were called Janna as well. *So* she named her own daughter Janna too. But her daughter changed her own name to Annie already when she was six years old. And after some hesitation, her parents agreed!

In those days, if someone wanted to know who Janna was, they said: "Who do you belong to?" The answer then was, "the Essinks." Later they would say to Annie: "What is your name?" She would then say, as young as she was, *"I'm Annie."*

165

The new question and the new answer are examples of individualization, of the growing independence of the person.

Janna went along to church and sat next to her parents and grandparents in the ancient family pew. And that was the way it should be. What way? The way of the tried and true (sub)cultural patterns, to which people conformed without objection.

She went to housekeeping school and then helped out at home on the farm. And that was the way it should be.

She professed her faith and was married "with the consent of his parents" to the son of a farmer who was a friend of the family — a nice, dependable, caring man. They had a good life together. And that was the way, and is often the way, it should be, if we are honest.

But for "I'm Annie" things turned out differently in her social class *for the first time in generations.* "Because that is the way it should be" was never sufficient reason for her to do or not to do something. Church, school, leisure time, career, marriage, children; *she did not simply conform.* She wanted to choose and decide herself.

And Janna let her become Annie. That is remarkable. She did it hesitantly, sometimes with fear and trembling. But she did it. *Because she probably realized that the time had finally come.*

Perhaps she had also wanted to be like that because of the time when we were young, about when the war ended. I remember that she was deliriously happy when she saw me standing as a soldier inside the cordon during the coronation celebration in '48. "I'm going to leave Drenthe," she called excitedly, and then she was pushed away with the stream of people.

She never got the chance. If I try to talk to her about it, she looks past me and changes the subject.

She is still conforming, not submitting — that is something quite different — but conforming. Fritz is right. She would have conformed to the pattern: the external center of marriage, the farm, always took first place. *If she and her foremothers had not conformed, they would never have survived as farmers.*

But now we live in another time, and her daughter can, thank God, afford the luxury of independence. Annie will therefore not accept that Fritz will not come to an understanding with her and will not reinvest in the double center of their marriage. And so she goes her own way. Not a very comprehensible way, mind you, since her friend is a tremendous bore, but that is not important here. "The daughter of Essink" and "I'm Annie" have a different self-consciousness. They are different people. That is what we are talking about here.

(The above is a typical country tale, although individualization proceeds at a faster pace in urban areas. But even there, I know that there are still [sub]cultures where the members are not or are little individualized.)

Annie Is Not a Sugar Cookie, but a Hazelnut Cake

As an illustration of this change of self-consciousness, I often use an old — in a certain sense corny — example from the bakery. Sugar cookies are shaped by a cookie cutter. The cookie cutter exists prior to the individual cookies. Their self-consciousness is the form that they derive from the cutter. Therefore they, of course, fit into the cookie box that has the same shape as the cutter, for which they were made.

Hazelnut cakes, in contrast, are made one by one, with a single nut in the middle. Their self-consciousness is also their form — round, unique, with that nut as center.

Thus they cannot simply fit into a mold. They can have all different kinds of shapes: circles, stars, ovals, and even shapes that look like sugar cookies.

And so the hazelnut cakes have *more* social possibilities than the sugar cookies, which are all cut from the same mold. But they are difficult to fit into the old cookie boxes, that were made for sugar cookies.

Not only love covenants suffer from this problem, but also, for example, church communities. And how!

There is a further problem with social institutions that work with immigrants. People from Turkey, for example, are all sugar cookies and therefore easily encounter problems here. Nearly all the social workers are, however, hazelnut cakes, who proceed on the assumption that everyone is just like them, or at least should be.

Oh, those young men and women do the best they can. Give them a break!

Over Time, Individualism Works Centripetally

Individualism has not advanced with the same strength everywhere; not everywhere within our countries, not in every area of life, not in all (sub)cultures. Nor could it, since the same accompanying factors were not present everywhere to everyone in the same way.

This creates a source of tension in all communities. Are we actually "part of" the community, or just "going along with" the community?

Those who were once "part of" something and have since become individualized always want to discuss everything endlessly before they decide whether they want to continue to go "along with it." Sometimes they even go so far as to want to discuss how they should discuss a certain subject. It can take a long time before a *code* is drawn up to deal with such problems more efficiently.

But those who are not individualized are, in the meantime, going crazy because they have not the foggiest idea what the problem is. And so communities are driven apart (e.g., churches!).

This centrifugal phenomenon can also be detected in marriages and other covenants and contracts. If they are made for reasons other than the Fire of Love, there is a reasonably good chance that they will not work out. If love is present, the two parties must be particularly vigilant and carefully "continue seeking" each other, if they want to keep the double center from collapsing.

Beck and Beck-Gernsheim make no distinction between covenants and contracts. In so doing they are, I think, too pessimistic. But they also overlook something else: *individualism seems to become, with time, a centripetal force,* because it puts people in a position independently to choose and decide for the other as such.

From One Dependency to Another?

The independence that lies at the basis of the described individualism always consists of two parts: a creative-intellectual part and a socio-economic part. If people possess one part, they try to acquire the other part as well (if, that is, there are enough factors present to assist them.)

Beck and Beck-Gernsheim point out that suddenly — at the end of the fifties and the beginning of the sixties — a great number of married

168

women realized "that the distance between them and poverty was only one man long." That is very possible. (That was also probably not the case, but rather they were attempting to acquire the socioeconomic part of independence. It is not only the very important question of financial independence, but primarily of full-fledged position.)

Women moved, therefore, en masse, into the *labor market*. For similar reasons, women already earlier had moved into the *education and training market*. Beck and Beck-Gernsheim see in this a chaos-producing factor — a centrifugal force, to put it in my own terms. Dependence on the man was exchanged for *dependence on the market*. Especially since the labor market makes difficult demands — such as "der oder die vollmobile Einzelne," the male or female fully mobile individual, who can be sent from here to there without any social or emotional attachments, who is available on demand and prepared to do any task, in accordance with what the market demands.

Today's labor market is totalitarian; it demands everything of a person. There is no place for people who have lovers to whom belong the first place. And so the labor market attempts to drive a wedge into the double center.

The education and training market has its own mechanism that can work centrifugally. Those who seek to forge independence via this market can even less afford themselves the luxury of a double center. "Study now, love later!" was perhaps an earlier solution. Those who want to achieve something nowadays give themselves over permanently to education, till death do them part. Those who have conformed to the traditional society have to break themselves away, but then fall prey immediately to the totalitarian and therefore inhuman market forces.

Negotiate or Seek Each Other

Once again I find Beck and Beck-Gernsheim too pessimistic.

What they maintain is, first of all, not valid for people with a love covenant, but for consumers who have closed a contract for mutual benefit. They must endlessly negotiate the place of residence (in the case of transfer or internship), the agenda (with changes in schedule), the division of household duties, having or not having children, use of the car, and a countless number of other details. Then it is constantly a question of toeing the middle line between "sticking up for oneself" and "being reasonable." That, in turn, can also become a source of conflict.

People who really love each other also face these same types of problems, but they do not negotiate like parties to a contract. They continue to *seek each other*. Thus they find solutions, and if these do not satisfy, they seek others. Because the beloved is above all things, and that is *mutual*.

Secondly, what Beck and Beck-Gernsheim say about exchanging one dependency for another is true for the *conformers*, but not for the individualists, as I view them: personable, self-conscious, independent, free, and responsible.

The women among them have not entered the labor or the education market in order to protect themselves against divorce, but because they have wanted to come into their own. The fact that they then no longer fit into a marriage or other relationship with someone who worked against them is a logical consequence of that.

"I'm Annie" does not take just anything anymore. She does not let go of hope; she lets go of her marriage instead. Why would people such as these now all of a sudden conform like sugar cookies to the expectations of the totalitarian market?

Narcissus w.d., the consumer, seeks his right through dependence. Shulamite believes, hopes, loves, and knows that her own right ultimately cannot be found in the market. She makes use of it, but only to the point that it is convenient for her.

> *What is a man, upright and true,*
> *in times like these supposed to do?*
> *He kisses his child, and then his wife,*
> *and goes to fight the idle fight.*

Is there any matter, any goal to which the double center of love may be subjected?
"No," I told Fritz. He thought that was irresponsible talk, and I promised to come back to it.

For that reason, the lines quoted above are taken from a poem that I still cannot read without being moved. It is by Jan Campert, and is called, "Het lied der achttien doden" (The song of the eighteen dead), which he wrote in 1941. ". . . We were eighteen in number, yet none

170

would see the evening."[1] After fifty years I still know it almost by heart.

Can I still maintain that the double center of love may not be subordinated to anything else?

It is my opinion that the man who is speaking in the poem is not sacrificing love to something higher. On the contrary, he invests his heart and soul in love. He does not overlook the everyday love either, like the eros of Plato would. It is not here a question of the higher, but of the trivial.

In those days it was love itself that was threatened by the henchmen of the empire of hate. So the man did what he could not avoid. He kissed his child and then his wife. For if evil had won, no one would have been able to love in freedom, least of all himself. ("... as surely as I soon shall die, my love no longer see, and no more break my bread with her or have her sleep near me. . . ." That is why he must do it, in order to secure all that.) That man loved his wife fervently. He did what he had to, and he was killed.

Now I dare to repeat it: there is nothing more important in life than love. Anyone who neglects the investment in the double center, no matter what the reason, harms himself and his lover and contributes to the demise of love.

Mein Kaiser, mein Kaiser

But public affairs are surely more important than personal interest?

After what has been said about the eighteen dead, this question is actually superfluous. The public good must be served, without a doubt, but not at the cost of the beloved. She comes first.

No one can really serve the public good if he allows his lover to languish. It is hopelessly cliché, but one must both do the one and not neglect the other.

No proud, independent lover needs to consider any affair of Caesar more important than his own double center.

That "of Caesar" is an allusion to another poem, this time of Heinrich Heine.[2] It is about two French Grenadiers, who are on the return

1. As found in *Geliefde gedichten,* ed. Wim Zaal (Amsterdam, 1972).
2. Found in many anthologies. The one used here is *Heinrich Heine,* ed. Willem Kloos (Amsterdam, 1906).

trip from Russia and then discover in Germany that their emperor, Napoleon Bonaparte, has been taken prisoner. The one wants to return immediately to his lover. The other has his mind on higher things:

> Was schert mich Weib, was schert mich Kind,
> Ich trage weit bessres Verlangen;
> Lasz sie bettln gehn, wenn sie hungrig sind —
> Mein Kaiser, mein Kaiser gefangen!

> What does my wife matter, what does my child matter,
> I bear far better yearnings;
> Let them go abegging when they are hungry —
> My Emperor, my emperor, a prisoner!

What a difference between these words and those of the one condemned to die in the song of Jan Campert. "Weit bessres Verlangen!" Far better yearnings indeed! If only I knew what side Heine was on.

Deus lo vult!

But the Platonists just do not give up that easily: "The things of *God*, then? Are they not higher and better than self-interest?"

First of all, investing in the double center is a far cry from self-interest. But we will let that go for now. The things of God are the things of little people; they are close by, found in normal, everyday life. (And from there they spread like an oil spill on water. From there.)

Those who truly want to serve the things of God walk along the way to Jericho past the wounded traveler, victim of thieves, toward the temple. They bear far better yearnings! But they understand nothing. Those who have no heart for their closest neighbor — their beloved — do not serve the things of God.

"But is it then not better for one man to suffer than that the whole people should perish?"

An important question. Caiphas, the high priest, asked it. Everyone nodded approvingly, and then with all good conscience had Jesus Christ crucified!

Who is not familiar with that stern church officer who pretends that

172

the coming of the Kingdom of Love depends entirely on his investment in the things of God and who in the meantime pays no attention to his wife and children? *Was schert mich Weib, was schert mich Kind?* God wills it! That is what they shouted nine hundred years ago in Clermont as well: "Deus lo vult!" With that began the frightening crusades, which opened wounds that still bleed today.

What God wills is Love. And it begins very close to home, in the everyday, normal interactions with our beloved one. Therefore, lovers of all lands, do not let yourselves be deceived by philosophers, businessmen, employers, professors, emperors, or high priests who want you to do their dirty work. Invest in the double center. From there everything is possible.

From the Double Center to the A-Circle: Children

A child has a very unique place in the we-circle system.

It begins in the womb, as a physical part of the double center as soon as it announces its presence, even before birth. At that moment, the whole system changes. Another one has come along who demands the necessary investment. In the beginning it is limited, but it gradually requires more, especially after it is born.

And so things cannot simply go on as they were before. The lovers must set aside their lifestyle. And they must continue to do so until the children are grown. (For other reasons as well, but we will discuss them later.)

The setting aside implies in this case that *more élan vital* must be invested in the double center, of which the child is at this point still an integral part. *That élan vital must come from somewhere.* Usually that is not a problem, because most people have some reserve. It is also often easy to find activities that can be cut back or completely eliminated. But with very active people it can be difficult. Then three mistakes are often made.

The first is that lovers free up élan vital by reducing their investment in each other. That is your worst solution; over the long haul that is most pernicious for the love covenant. The élan vital necessary for the (coming) child must derive from the length or the breadth, but under no circumstances must it be taken from the double center.

The second mistake is that the man in no way alters his lifestyle and becomes a sort of "absent father" who leaves everything to his wife and is only available for consultation in emergencies. And by then he has not a clue as to what it is all about.

In the meantime, the woman must unilaterally give up a number of activities, among which are not only activities that she "had," but also activities that she "was"; that belonged to her ego and even touched her heart. As a result, she suffers from ego-loss, having lost a piece of herself. In order to find herself again, she should actually go through an élan vital–draining grieving process, but she cannot, because of the baby . . . etc.

The third easy mistake to make is that neither one cuts back their activities and they become exhausted. That will, in the long run, cost the love of the child.

The best solution is that both consciously cut back or cut out activities that do not belong to their egos and do not touch their hearts. That is not done by means of "negotiation," but by seeking each other. Renouncing one's membership may very well produce objections and angry faces at the bridge club or the gym, but that cannot be avoided. Every club or group has a tendency to try to keep itself in existence and thus handles deserters roughly.

The above turns out very differently in situations of material poverty. It is not as generalized as it was before, when many men had to invest all their élan vital in their work in order to support the family. But poverty unfortunately still exists — and not least among those who have far too high a mortgage on their far too luxurious house.

The Child as External Center

That the child can also become an external center has already been noted. When this happens, the lovers hardly invest anything in the double center anymore, and direct all their energies toward the children. In fact, they cease to be lovers with children and become instead parents. (I had an uncle and aunt who consistently called each other father and mother, even when the children were not around.)

The phenomenon is very understandable. The unborn and the recently born child make up an integral part of the double center. Investing in each other includes, for a time at least, investing in the child. If by

174

virtue of circumstances, or by virtue of improper division, there remains little élan vital, almost unconsciously the entire flow is directed definitively toward the child. It becomes their "everything." They "live for their child."

To this must be added that children have a very special *central meaning* for their parents and create a very special *central experience*. It is incomparable. They are the life of our life, and more than that. They justify our hope in the future. (That can take on very demeaning forms if the children must achieve what their parents were not able to achieve. But that remains beyond our scope.)

A person is nowhere so vulnerable as in his or her children. It is thus no wonder that children easily take the place of the double center.

We often see that happen with a handicapped child, who needs special care. That is also especially true for mothers who have no (longer) other central meanings or experiences, and whose husbands are "absent fathers." That can produce a very problematic, asymmetrical relationship.

Children should never, as external center, take the place of the double center — for the sake of love, but also for the sake of the children.

Parental love has an essential condition: that it point away from itself. Even before the child is born and is therefore still part of the mother's body, it is still "someone else." It must be displaced from the double center in order to be able to return as a member of the A-circle. *The nuclear family must replace itself as an extended family.* (The relationship between parents and adult children, however, never becomes completely symmetrical. Children entrust themselves less and less to their parents and vice versa.)

Whoever tries to hold on to a child will lose it. First it must leave the womb — that creates pain and difficulty — then it must leave the crib, the playpen, the backyard, and finally it must leave sight. So it proceeds, always with pain and difficulty, up to the moment that it goes out the door and takes the rudder of life in hand.

But that creates great problems if the child has become the external center of (one of) the parents. Then the child is held on to rather than sent off. It must pull itself loose, sometimes with violence, and then the return as member of the extended family becomes very difficult. Or, even worse, it permits itself to be clung to.

We will not elaborate that any further. This is not a book on child-rearing.

175

Centrifugally Working Children

Usually children are natural talents at keeping parents together. They even resort to magic.

But they can also, willingly or unwillingly, work centrifugally to drive the double center apart.

That is especially the case with the so-called *solidarity breakers.* They are foster or step-children who, out of solidarity with their former parent(s), make a completely normal chaos out of the new situation.

Sometimes that is not at all difficult. There are couples with three or more different types of children in their lives, from former marriages (or something resembling marriage) and from the current marriage. With those who are divorced, continual arrangements have to be made with "ex-partners" concerning visitation, problems at school, purchases, vacations. It must all be regulated so that no one comes up short. In and of itself that often causes great tension and reopens old wounds. If, on top of it all, the children then have problems with their double loyalties and begin to make trouble, circumstances can become so complicated that everyone is at odds with everyone, including themselves.

But even when that is not the case, solidarity breakers try to centrifuge the double center, under mottoes like, "things *did* not work out with my real father; thus things *will* not work out with this one." One ought not hold it against them, but the intrigues of the court of Louis XIV were parlor games compared to what some of the solidarity breakers are capable of. One cannot resolve such cases without professional help. But that again devours élan vital.

I think it is a remarkable phenomenon. If there are problems with the children — whatever they may be — the lovers must invest *more* in their loving interaction in order to hold fast to one another and to muster enough élan vital to conquer the problems. More time, more care, more tenderness, more frequent and longer walks hand in hand, an extra cup of tea in bed. Those kinds of common, essential details. But instead, what usually happens? The first thing they do is pay less attention to each other.

"I just can't think about it right now."

"But your heart is crying out for it, and hers even more."

"Ah, it will work out later."

Let's hope so, but it is very, very risky behavior.

Cracks Can Also Work Centrifugally

The old patterns of loving interaction have for the most part become unusable in today's world, and the new are not yet available. That wreaks havoc, especially when a problem arises between the lovers for which there is no obvious solution.

Traditionally that was handled by means of the existing division of labor ("I will not concern myself with that") or from the existing lines of authority ("if it comes to that point, I am the boss here"). But now the division of labor is no longer fixed and the lines of authority no longer exist. People are often forced by circumstances to reach for strategies that may work well enough outside of love, but that simply do not apply inside the love relationship.

"*We* have a *problem* for which we will certainly find a solution," then becomes "*She* and *I* have a *conflict.*" Then comes the first round of conflict resolution, straight out of the manual for new members of the labor board.

First accentuate the differences, because nothing may be glossed over. Then place the differing points of view over against each other. And finally, negotiate a compromise. (That can be done well or poorly.) If that does not work, take radical action; find out who can hold their breath the longest. This course of action evokes feelings that are so completely foreign to those who participate in the osmotic we-experience that both end up utterly out of breath and wondering what has come over them.

They do not recognize each other. No, most likely not.

They have unawares and unwillingly wandered off into the consumer world of Narcissus w.d., where ultimately only self-interest matters; or perhaps even into the hunting grounds of Eros w.d., who uses power and violence if he does not get his way.

"You don't love me anymore!" No, it does not seem much like it during such a scene.

But be careful. In fact, they are probably simply lost. If that is the case, they will easily find their way back, *and from that point on they will love each other even more* and will be able to laugh about it with only slight embarrassment. "We should never let that happen again."

They had temporarily lost their good self-consciousness during the fight. And so they said things and did things that revealed not the true

177

nature of the mosaic, but the cracks. That should not happen too often, for in the panic to rid themselves of each other, and to reduce each other to powerlessness, irreparable damage can be caused. If the cracks are revealed too often and too clearly, they have a centrifugal effect. Or, to use another metaphor, if I look into the mirror of the other and I too often see an image in which I do not recognize myself, I either begin to believe it is me, or I turn away from it for the sake of self-preservation.

Reconciliation

How can such frightening deviations into the love-void regions be avoided?

Some do not want to avoid them at all. On the contrary, they think that the storms that blow in those parts are necessary to purify love. *In my opinion,* that is an erroneous and dangerous thought, although it is very old, probably going all the way back to Heraclitus.

If the air needs to be cleared, I can think of a much better method — *reconciliation.* It takes place entirely within the garden of Shulamite. Mutually seeking each other's true nature, always prepared to grant each other credit, nothing glossed over or accentuated. The difficulties are experienced as *our* problems, that *we* must resolve, together. "We will get through this somehow, my love."

The difficulties, the irritation, even the pain and the fighting lie completely within the realm of love now. When seen in this light, reconciliation is an investment and a renewal of the love covenant.

That is the only good way to handle it! Do not be fooled by the devotees of Heraclitus, Hegel, and Marx. They do not have a good perspective on love.

Yet we all know that it is difficult for lovers to avoid the dangerous zones. They have to (want to) learn, and must afterward calmly review where and how they managed to lose their way.

Sometimes it seems to be a matter of one of the earlier mentioned defensive reactions. They must then be taken into account. (Or treated externally, if one absolutely cannot live with them anymore. But one should not make that decision too hastily. Defensive reactions are the raisins in the bread of character, but sometimes there is indeed a stone among them.)

178

More frequently, however, it is just a question of a lack of available élan vital for the double center. What also plays a surprisingly big role is the bodily condition: tiredness, lack of sleep, bad or irregular eating habits, drinking too much, slight feelings of malcontent due to normal, periodic fluctuations or to an as of yet undetected sickness. Everyone has, where this is concerned, shifting limits, and it is up to the lover to be continually aware of them. Trendy psychologizing has never produced anything of benefit.

Disagreement, Tension, and Revolt Work Centripetally

In love, the word *disagreement* is often viewed, without justification, as something that must be avoided at all costs.

That is a carryover from the time when the lover was a derivation of the other. At that time, the double center was still depicted as a circle with one single middle point. Now it is an ellipse with two foci, not one, but two (at least if the modern fusers do not try to make them into a single point again).

People who are given to each other, and have found each other, can continue to seek each other dialogically only if they are and remain other. That necessarily creates *tension,* another word with an undeserved negative meaning. A love covenant that does not contain some tension is ready for remodeling. It is like a bow. If there is not good tension, you cannot shoot very far with it. Lack of tension is just as dangerous as too much tension.

The third word mentioned in the list was *revolt.* To revolt against something that is in conflict with proper respect for the true nature of someone or something is *an act of love.* If I find that my lover in some way or other is being unfair to me, and I simply put up with it in the name of peace or the like, then I am selling myself short *and her too.*[3]

Those who cannot revolt against themselves or the other either begin to hate or become resigned. The second is almost worse than the first, but in both cases, they are beyond the garden of Shulamite.

3. Rebellion and rebelliousness belong together. The "right of rebellion" and the "duty to rebel" are old Calvinistic principles — the Dutch state owes its origin to them. It is unclear to me why these same principles were not applied when it came to the Calvinistic concept of husband-wife relationships.

A-Circle: The Loved Ones

Around the double center there lies a broad circular band that can be called the A-circle. In that band we find what I call the beloved ones. They are the ones who stand closest to us, who touch our hearts, about whom we care a great deal, whom we love, whom we mourn when they are no longer with us. These and other like expressions point to a covenant, since we are dealing with the other as such and not with any benefit or advantage.

The A-circle is of greatest importance for lovers. If they claim that they need no one and nothing else, they are necessarily making a big mistake. First, the A-circle keeps the double center from *overheating.* The warmth of the fire must be dissipated somehow. Second, this A-circle protects the double center like a shield from the cold, merciless world.

The A-circle is also established through interaction. It is, in essence, qualitatively and quantitatively *different* from the loving interaction of the double center.

The reason for this is the decided devotion of Shulamite. She creatively alters reality. "You are an apricot tree in the midst of thorn bushes." Thus it is clear: the interaction with the apricot tree cannot help but be different than the interaction with the thorns.

In the A-circle, therefore, the nature and extent of the mutual entrusting is different and less than that of the double center. The depth is different and less, and the investment is different and less in terms of time, place, and treatment.

Nevertheless, the A-circle lies so close to the double center that there is a danger of supplanting and encroachment. We will come back to that, but for now let it suffice to say that the borders must be carefully guarded. Not for reasons of principle, but for practical reasons. The borders between the other we-circles are less clear, more permeable, and are more interchangeable the farther one gets from the double center.

Members of the A-Circle

We have already spoken of the special position that children hold in the A-circle. This is also the circle of intimate friends, and for certain family members, but definitely not all of them. The modern person chooses and decides who will belong to the A-circle.

The members of the A-circle who are not one's own offspring must be carefully selected. One cannot simply entrust everything to everyone who happens to be in the neighborhood. Allegiance must be evident.

Those who carelessly grant access to the A-circle and a position close to the double center often end up feeling threatened. Under the influence of alcohol or an artificially intimate atmosphere, it too often happens in conversation that we confide too much. We then run the risk that it will later be used against us, or that it will be spread on the street. ("You should hear what he said about his wife!")

In the choice of our intimate friends, we must be careful. Once we have them, we must interact gently with them, because we need them.

It often happens that couples with grown children seem not to need anyone else. The children and their friends are always an imposing presence during the weekends. And in between, they still know how to keep their parents busy. Everyone thinks it is great.

But then the moment arrives when the children move out, buy their own washing machines, work in their own gardens, and want to form their own circles.

Suddenly the parents are alone, and discover not only that their nest is empty, but that their A-circle is too, and that it is not easy at their age to build a trustworthy relationship quickly. Then they begin to lean on the children.

Fragmentation

Parents who want to keep their families together, or who want to act like their family still exists, have the tendency to push their children to admit each other into their A-circles in order to form an A-circle community.

In and of itself that is very understandable, because until recently, it was still the case that we-circles were preestablished and that people simply conformed to them. The people with whom one lived usually came from families who knew each other and were related to each other in various ways through marriage. *People interacted with each other day and night.* They worked, lived, loved, celebrated, and mourned with each other.

The individualization and the mobility that gave rise to it have put an end to this situation. Life is completely fragmented. The people with

181

whom we live are often other than those with whom we work, and other than those with whom we play sports, and again other than those with whom we go to the theater or church — where applicable.

Our family members often no longer belong within this conglomeration. They are spread all over the country and all over the world. The continuity of interaction with them is broken.

We can do something about that through family gatherings, letter-writing, and telephone contact, but all this does not prevent — unless there were very close ties in the past — alienation between close family members. They often become members of B- or C-circles, with a certain mutual feeling of guilt. In order to alleviate that feeling, we often look for a stick with which to beat the dog. And we can usually find one.

A-Interaction

The loving interaction of the double center is characterized by the fact that people have the tendency — which they sometimes feel obliged to follow — "always to do everything, everywhere, deeply, together."

The A-interaction is characterized by the tendency toward "*often*, but not always; *a lot,* but not everything; *lots of places,* but not everywhere; *trustingly,* but not too deeply." (Moreover, it is accompanied by the difference in quality mentioned above between the interaction with the apricot tree and the thorn bushes.)

This way of describing the A-interaction offers the possibility of a number of practical instructions. The first is that the A-circle must have a limited character, otherwise it is impossible to muster the necessary élan vital. Then one continually feels that he "really ought to do something again" with everyone and yet never feels that he has done enough.

"We must not disappoint our good friends, Marie."

No, we should not, but in the meantime he and Marie never have an evening or weekend to relax with each other. That can lead to no good.

The modern person chooses and decides whom to grant access to her A-circle. She no longer conforms to preestablished patterns. Very good. But if she is not aware of her limitations, she makes an overwrought mess of the whole thing, and no one is happy.

The second is the already mentioned danger of supplanting and/or encroachment. "A lot, but not everything," "often, but not always" . . . those are very flexible instructions.

The double center and the A-circle can, more or less unnoticed, begin to overlap each other. "Those people are far too close to each other," it is called in popular parlance. They do — with one or more of their friends — nearly everything, almost everywhere, nearly all the time, and very deeply — or a select combination of one or more of these.

One confidence leads easily to another, and that usually leads, among people of the same erotic type, to sex. "We are just celebrating friendship!" someone once cheerfully said to me, and that struck me as a convenient discovery.

Eros w.d. thinks it is great and Narcissus w.d. will go along as long as it does not become a burden to him, but Shulamite cannot bear it. She is jealous, because she is monogamous. *Could she maybe?* Can she not still decidedly and creatively devote herself to her apricot tree?

"But surely it does not have to be that way, Will!"

Maybe not, but I have never experienced anything else, although it is of course always possible that I have simply had a bad time of it. Some people say that there are lovers who are able to manage it, but I do not know of any. For practical reasons, for the sake of Shulamite, I plead with you. Do not let the interaction of the double center overlap (unnoticed) with that of the A-circle.

The Church and the Tennis Club

Another unfortunate result of fragmentation is that all kinds of organizations — institutions, functions of society — discover that their individualized members no longer form a community, since they no longer interact with each other day and night.

That results in a loosely related band of consumers, who do not feel responsible for each other or for the whole. These people never want positions of responsibility and quickly disappear if something does not agree with them.

Because of their unique character, church groups in particular have problems with this. If individualized people really want to choose and decide before they "join" and stay, *then there must be some kind of experience*

183

at the A-level of fellowship, minimally B-level. The traditional, formal church service is inadequate for that.

And so it is sought in smaller interest or project groups. But before anything can be truly experienced, there must be a substantial dose of mutual trust. *This is not something that individualized people automatically grant, since they usually do not even know each other, much less have A- or B-interaction during the week.*

And so something more than just talk must take place: actions, celebrations, meals, hikes, a creative afternoon together with the children, visiting with each other, weekend retreats, a newsletter. (Many events, in different places, frequently, and for enough duration, so that the heart is reached.) All good things. Community building, that is called. But such a church group must lay an almost totalitarian claim to the lives of its participants. They impose a number of people on their A- and B-circles and also a number of élan vital–absorbing activities.

"We have to, if we love the church, Marie; you cannot avoid everything."

But in the meantime the board of the tennis club has caught on and has decided that something must be done in order to shore up the straggly band, so that the members will behave less like consumers and will feel more responsibility for the club. And so: fundraisers for the building, and then for the starving children in Zambia, parties, barbecues, dances, scavenger hunts, creative afternoons with the children, visiting each other, weekend retreats, and a club newspaper.

All good things. Such a club is, after all, a function of a community. *If the community*—because it no longer exists in its original form—*no longer forms the club, the club must, if it wants to continue to exist, form its own community.*

Again, a totalitarian claim with a number of imposed A- and B-circle members.

"But we have to, if we love tennis, Marie. You cannot . . ." Nope, not that either.

The school board cannot be outdone in such an individualized new neighborhood. The school too must form its own community in order to stay in existence: fundraisers, parties, church services, sport days, scavenger hunts, barbecues, discussion groups, commissions. . . .

The music society organizes nature walks while the nature club organizes musical evenings. Members are continually divided up into small groups in order to enhance mutual contact, but no one is ever placed in a group with one's lover.

If our lover is our love, if our beloved ones are our beloved ones, these types of totalitarian claims must be checked — they are too similar to those of the labor and education markets.

There the ideal is the "vollmobile Einzelne," the fully mobile individual. Here, with institutions, the ideal is the "gevestigde Einzelne," the settled individual, without love and without A- and B-circles. These will be provided by the institution, as was formerly done by the traditional community.

My conclusion is that here too lovers must take control of their own lives in order to have time for themselves, each other, and their chosen beloved ones: establish boundaries.

If they are unable, or dare not establish boundaries, they must not complain about love when they lose each other and their beloved ones, in spite of all that they have found, and everything that was given to them.

An Aside

Then what must we then do with institutions, functions of a society that have changed in nature?

That is not at all the issue here. Here we are dealing with the Restoration of Love. Surely we need not resolve the problems of the church and the tennis club before we may love? Let the institutions renew themselves.

That does occur from time to time and there are, roughly speaking, two extreme models and a number of mediating forms of renewal.

The one extreme is the commercialization (the sports club model). The members are consumers and simply pay for services, which are then provided by paid professionals.

The other extreme is a sort of new segregation (the yacht club model, "our kind" of people). The members are completely involved and limit their we-circle and their institution to a smaller, supervisor A- and B-community.

One of the possible mediating forms is that a group of

completely involved members found an institution, and then very wisely choose for the commercial model (the AAA model).

The A1-Circle: The Beloved Ones

Not only people are beloved to people. Also beloved are animals, plants, things, and circumstances, among them especially the workplace — in short, nature and culture.

I call that the A1-circle, that to which people are attached and to which their heart goes out. What a central meaning it has in their life and what a central experience it invokes has already been mentioned. Lovers knew beforehand how much it meant in their lives and they have chosen it, even if it must be kept "separate," or completely "outside."

But just as the A-circle is not stable — people come and go and others change position — so too the A1-circle is a dynamic whole. Suddenly whole worlds can open up whose mere existence was never before suspected.

Here too the borders must be well guarded, especially with enthusiastic and rather excessive types. Even worse, from time to time one or both can be completely absorbed by The Beloved.

Then we are not dealing with some Sacred Duty, Mein Kaiser, The Business, or the like, but something that the lover indeed loves. *Someone who becomes completely absorbed in something is unfaithful to himself and to his lover.* The other must remain the other; the beloved other too.

"One day I just discovered that I was married to a puppeteer," a woman once said to me. That does not hold water. No one can have a puppeteer, swimmer, stamp collector, flautist, or doctor as lover. They may populate the A1-circle . . . then we can talk about puppets, swimming, etc.

Everything that we have said about excess and encroachment applies here as well in a somewhat different way.

"But life is so short, there is so much to experience and reality is so exciting," the puppeteer and the doctor said to me.

My answer was that I would be the last to deny it, but that *it all seems so small and boring compared to what can be experienced with one's lover. The best is yet to come.* If the lovers continue to seek each other. That's for sure.

186

Wider Circles

The B-circle contains, let us say, friends and acquaintances, good neighbors. People who are known by their first name, and whom we "run into" every once and a while. Those who show up at birthday parties and with whom we occasionally do other things as well: dining, walks, "something nice." Some lay close to the A-circle, others close to the C-circle; the broader circles are also dynamic.

With the B-circle there is a considerable degree of mutual trust. If it is betrayed, it is painful. If they disappear, they are missed.

The B-circle can be wider than the A-circle, but too wide is not good either. Then people again run short of élan vital for the A-circle and the double center. There is, moreover, an analogical B1-circle. And so forth. But we know all that by now.

And yet it is not superfluous to pause here for a moment, since there are those who underestimate the importance of the B-circle. The breadth of their love then becomes too small. Their sun has too little room to shine and to be reflected. Their moon catches too few rays from others, and if they end up in the cold, they have too little protection.

The C-circle could be called the circle of casual acquaintances, and the D-circle that of people whose names we know and with whom we occasionally make superficial conversation. The E-circle contains those whose faces we recognize and whom we vaguely greet on the street. And the F-circle are those unknown people whom we see from time to time on the street and with whom we exchange a smile or a look of understanding over an incident that we have both witnessed, or to whom we might even say a friendly word.

They belong to the outermost region of personal love. They are also indispensable, since they are designed for our love, and we for theirs.

Precise divisions and distinctions do not add a lot to it. But something must be said. For adults, and especially for children who enter a strange environment, the vague greeting and the superficial conversation are indispensable signs of hope. When the exchange of a smile, a look of understanding, and a friendly word with strangers and foreigners is no longer possible, the light of a society is quenched.

A Life of Their Own

Lovers have a life of their own. That was already true before individualization penetrated deeply into all levels of society. Already then they had not only their own separate worlds of imagination, meaning, and experience, but also their own, separate activities. "Because Adam, he will work, and Eve will do the wash," my mother revealingly sang as she stood with her hands in the hot, soapy water in the tub.

"Isn't washing work too, Mama?"

No, no. Real work in those days in Drenthe only took place on the farms and in the factories. The rest was just a bunch of easy tasks that deserved no name. And so my father did not work, although he was away from home all day at his easy tasks, and returned home dead tired from them. My mother also had her hands full. There was little or no élan vital for anything else.

In these times much has changed. I consider that gain for the individual, for the personal self-realization, and therefore for love.

It is gain because there is *more élan vital* available to express in time, place, and action. It need not all be applied to acquiring one's daily bread. *Thus a man no longer need be a derivative of his work, and the woman no longer need be a derivative of her man.*

If they approach things somewhat efficiently, there is enough élan vital left over that they can both have their own life.

Elan vital is like money. It is only given once. Whoever does not think things through soon spends it on unprofitable things without ever really deriving any satisfaction for their money.

Money for spending must be well *distributed.* Not long ago at a fiftieth wedding anniversary I heard people snickering about the fact that the bride had always said: "We have two kinds of money: Ours and mine." (In most cases it would have been the opposite.)

In order to maintain love, there must *three kinds* of élan vital: Ours, yours, and mine.

Another Pansy

That means that in each situation it must be decided how the household duties can most efficiently be arranged. If Eve goes to work, Adam must do the wash, and if they both work, they both must do the wash. It is unbelievable that people who claim to love each other still make a fuss about this in this day and age. We have already had this discussion, I think.

It is of primary importance for love that in the distribution of the extra élan vital enough is reserved "for us." That should be spent — with a clear understanding of boundaries — on the double center and on the joint we-circle, as we already said. What "enough" is will remain for the moment beyond our scope.

It is, secondly, just as important that *both* lovers receive a proportional amount that they can spend — separately — on the education or labor markets and in their own we-circles, including what they consider beloved, or nice to do or to have.

What lovers weave — *separately* — in terms of acquaintances, experiences, skills, and things, comes back into the double center and cannot help but have an enriching effect on the loving interaction. That which in this case is done "separately" is actually done in a certain sense "for us." Otherwise it becomes a portion of extra élan vital that is spent *outside* of love. We are talking here about friends, skills, experiences, and things that one will not, cannot, may not, or dare not bring to the lover.

There is always some of that: portions of a course, details at work, confidential conversations with members of the A- or B-circle, experiences with nature or culture that the other just has no sensitivities for.

An *own life* as *separate life* is necessary and must be stimulated by the other.

A life of one's own, as that which may be kept *outside* of love, is inevitable, but must be as restricted as possible.

A life of one's own that not only is kept outside of love, but is even a *hidden or secret life*, works centrifugally and must be avoided.

Those who are unable to separate themselves from it irretrievably lose their lover, and that is the worst thing that can happen to Shulamite. So pay attention, fools!

189

The Fire Is the Measure

That "enough" élan vital must be invested in the double center has been repeatedly stated.

But what is the measure of "enough"? "Everything" is too much; then things *overheat*, that is clear. "Nothing" is too little; then the fire goes out.

The measure can be none other than the fire; better said, Love's Fire.

We all know our own symptoms of being in love best. The shiver down the spine as we see our lover approaching in the distance, the happy confidence as we walk hand in hand through the rain, singing silly songs together in the car, the need to be alone with her and to go everywhere with her, the security and the expectation, complete with little fits of panic: "I do not disappoint you, do I?" "Disappoint me? You? What makes you think that?" "Thank God."

If that kind of silliness — or some completely different kind — begins to weaken or disappear, if a certain irritability appears that cannot be traced to any particular incident, if after a reconciliation there remains something amiss — in short, if the fire is burning less brightly, there is too little élan vital being invested in the double center.

It is senseless to begin to psychologize about this. The only good answer is invest *more. More, not less,* as some do. More and other basic forms of loving interaction, more frequently and longer, more deeply and in more places.

Where must that élan vital come from? Who cares? It must just happen, and *quickly* too.

Not only quickly, but also *fundamentally.* Those who discover that Love's Fire has begun to smolder must structurally readjust their lives. A nice weekend together is not enough. They must live differently.

Sometimes the need for readjustment is clear to everyone — for example, when expecting a baby, as we saw before. But there are not only clear changes in existence, but also small, incremental changes. They cause a person one day to discover that for quite some time now things have not been so nice as they were at first.

Readjust quickly and fundamentally, then, but also with a certain optimistic *tenacity.*

There are two reasons for this. The first is that each (necessary) reorganization first causes disorganization. In other words: *with readjust-*

190

ment things get worse before they get better. When wallpapering a room, everyone finds that to be true. But when our love life is due for a tune-up, everything has to be back in order just like that. Otherwise people lose courage.

The second reason is that of the *delayed effect.* Only a hard whack with a sledgehammer has immediate effect. All other results make us wait a little longer.

Experience teaches us such readjustments of the pattern of investment always require at least six weeks before the flames of Love's Fire are burning brightly again. For each week that one has failed to make the proper investment, two weeks are necessary to revive it.

10. Basic Forms

Indissoluble

Lovers have at their disposal a number of basic dialogical forms for their loving interaction. Each one of them is an indispensable means of keeping the fire burning. They are touching, caring, meals, playing, dreaming, travel, work, glances, words, and celebrations. (The last, strictly speaking, does not really belong in this list.)

(That these same basic forms can be used to make life miserable for each other goes without saying. Looks cannot only inspire life, but can also kill. Words can caress and cut. That is the dark side. But we are not talking about that anymore.)

None of the basic forms may be lacking. They are an indissoluble whole for lovers, even though it sometimes appears that they can be taken apart. Years ago I more or less placed them under this rubric and gave them a name.[1] It had to be so at the time in order to make clear to verbally proficient intellectuals that there are often better means available in orthopedagogy than words.

An Aside

The way in which lovers make use of these basic forms is rather complicated. Not only has communication science lent it much

1. See my *Het herstel van het gewone leven* [The restoration of the common life] (Groningen, 1988) and *Over troosten en verdriet* [On comfort and grief] (Kampen, 1991).

attention in recent years, but so has semiotics,[2] that is, the science of "signs" that people give each other in order to make clear what it is they want to communicate.

An important semiotic distinction is that which is made between *signals* and *symptoms*. Both are signs. The difference is that signals are used purposefully while symptoms are unconsciously present.

If people want to leave the impression that they are good-natured, they will signal this with a smile, yet, perhaps without realizing it, the symptom of balled fists is also present.

The symptom is therefore often more revealing than the signal. That is often called "body language," but not entirely correctly. By means of intensive interaction, one quickly comes to realize whether the signals agree with the symptoms. "The morning after the night before" has shed much light on this subject.

Another important distinction is made between *demonstrative* and *referential* signs. The first are signs that refer to a specific thing in fixed circumstances. These are the signs of Eros.

My wife glances at the thermometer and says, "It is only sixty-three degrees in here." This demonstrative sign can also have the additional *connotation* of "Would you please turn up the thermostat?"

People who always make their intentions known in an indirect manner, through connotations, often make too great a demand on the intuitive capabilities of others and are therefore easily offended.

"It sure is nice weather," he says.

That is a demonstrative sign. But perhaps his connotation is that he would like to go fishing, work in the garden, or go for a bike ride with her. He would do better to make that clear by means of another demonstrative sign. But maybe not, if he only wants to throw out the possibility to see whether she will come to the same conclusion and wants to avoid her rejecting the idea out of hand or agreeing without really wanting to.

2. See Eco, Droste, Sebeok, and Barthes in the bibliography.

Part of "seeking the lover" is developing a certain sensitivity for such possible connotations.

Referential signs point to something that lies beyond the circumstances. There are two types: hermeneutic and symbolic. A hermeneutic reference points to a meaning, or to an experience of the senses or the ego. Narcissus cannot be without these types of signs. He gives her five roses. But his is not a demonstrative sign, along the lines of, "Put them in a vase . . . beautiful flowers, not too expensive today." He wants to say something else with them, because he has access to her worlds of meaning and experience, and he knows that roses play a role in those worlds, especially today, especially five roses today.

He does not mean that as a connotation, but rather purposefully. This is also the way in which lovers seek and find each other.

A hermeneutic sign thus refers not to anything specific, in the concrete circumstance, but still to something *known*.

The symbolic sign (symbolic in the semiotic sense), on the other hand, refers — straight through the circumstances, meaning, and the experience of the sense and the ego — to the mysterious, the secret, the wonder of it all. In connection with this book, to the wonder of love. It is the most important sign of Shulamite.

The rose, as a demonstrative, erotic sign can be *touched, seen, and smelled*. As a referential, hermeneutical, narcissistic sign, the rose can be *lived and experienced*.

The rose as a referential, symbolic, Shulamithic sign causes the lovers to *become aware* of something in their hearts. It reveals by concealing and conceals by revealing the true nature of the rose, of love, of each other. Osmosis with each other and the fullness of reality. Peak experiences, all systems go, etc.

Code and Kairos

The code of a love covenant usually contains, among other things, unspoken agreements on how one normally handles the basic forms: *what* the lovers do with each other, *how deeply* they do it, *what signs* they use, *when*, and *how often*.

194

These are set codes, where little is left to improvisation and spontaneity, but which guarantee a good measure of predictability. Thorndike was a proponent of this.

"No matter what happens, I can always count on the fact that, whether he feels like it or not, Jon will have the house in order and supper ready when I come home tired from classes." (That can be nothing other than one of Jon's designated signs. It can also refer to the meaning that she has given it. It could also be a *ritual*. Then it also points to a mystery. We will return to this later.)

There are also informal codes, with little predictability. "See, do, whatever you want." That lies more in the line of Rousseau. Both Thorndike and Rousseau have a point. Lovers need a code with a number of fixed, predictable signs, and yet room for the unexpected, the spontaneous, the improvised.

The lovers themselves will determine the meaning. If one or both are not happy with the code, it is silently broken, and the lovers find each other again — if everything goes well, at least. To that must be added that many modern couples underestimate the centripetal force of a set code.

It is my conviction that *all* the basic forms in a code are proper. That lovers must strive for *depth* goes without saying at this point. But *when*, and *how often?*

If this is encoded in an informal way, it seems that a number of basic forms normally get neglected and that in their place other routine, hurried, and superficial forms are used.

Connected to this is the feeling that depth cannot be encoded. That depends on the *kairos,* the *golden moment,* which comes suddenly and must be taken advantage of immediately, because otherwise it disappears.

It comes suddenly, that unexpected, golden moment, but *it does not just happen*. It does not come if there is no more élan vital left; it does not come if the next appointment has already arrived, and if the basic forms must be run through like an obligatory routine while the mind is on something else. Nor does it come if the bedroom is the only place where the lovers attempt to experience something with each other.

The unexpected comes only if part of the lovers' code is that they *regularly* take *time* for just the two of them to do *various things, in various places; things that they both enjoy.*

195

All of a Sudden, but Not Just Like That

"It started, I think, with the dishes. The younger ones were already in bed, and our oldest was at a friend's house. Bert saw that the faucet was leaking and went to get a pliers to tighten it up. At first it didn't work. He stood back, mumbling softly to himself, and then he looked at me and laughed.

"That was not it yet, but almost.

"We continued doing the dishes and talking; I don't remember what we talked about now, but I do remember that we understood each other.

"Then I sat down to read and he cleaned up his things. He was singing to himself as he did, and I sat singing along in the chair in the living room. Then it was quiet in the kitchen.

"Suddenly it was there. I am not sure how to describe it. You call it the Golden Moment, I believe. I understood how terribly much I loved him and felt that we should *do* something right away.

"Then the doorbell rang. What a shame! I no longer could hear Bert, so I went and opened the front door.

"There he stood with an odd bunch of flowers in his hand. He had gone out the back door and had picked them in the dark from the garden. 'Good evening, Miss,' he said shyly, while he fussed with the flowers. 'I have come to invite you to accompany me to the city tomorrow, first to eat, and then to see the second show.'

"'Well, Sir. This is somewhat unexpected,' I said, 'I will have to ask my mother first. But do please come in for a moment. What lovely flowers you have there. Are they for me?'

"That was such a fun evening, a lovely night and a lovely week.

"I dried the flowers. They did not turn out very well, but the bunch of stems still hangs next to our bed. It is so wonderful to love someone!"

A romantic fairy tale? Not at all! Just hard reality. Clear. That is for sure. Very clear.

Touch

If two lovers touch each other in some way, then it should be erotic. Chapter 6 says some things on this subject.

If two lovers touch each other and there is no trace of an erotic feeling, then something is wrong. Either they are on the way to losing each other — and then a quick attempt must be made to reconcile — or there is something else that has caused a loss of vegetative pressure.

Meta-erotic

The loss of pressure can be caused by the body, in the broadest sense of the word, thus including states of depression.

It can also be that the lovers share some great concern or grief. But as with sickness, they still desire to touch each other, in order gently and intimately to share the inexpressible. They are then, however, beyond the erotic — either temporarily or for good.

That is *meta-erotic,* the opposite of investment erotic. It is the dividend paid out on the investment. The investment must have first taken place, of course, and not simply by means of a superficial and hasty release of vegetative pressure in bed. If things have gone well, the lovers have attained a refined sense of each other's body signs (signals, symptoms, connotations, indications, references). That is always indispensable, but especially when there are no more words to say; after a calamity, during the critical or terminal stage of an illness, with aphasia or dementia. Lovers are able at that point to continue the dialogue of their love on a meta-erotic level and to be "happy in spite of it all."

"The Cat Gets More Strokes Than I Do"

They were young and wanted to discuss their situation, because things were not going so well, they thought, and they found it difficult to speak civilly to each other about it. And so they spoke to me, and I managed to maneuver things so that they were actually speaking to each other. After two or three sessions they did not need me anymore.

197

They found it difficult to express themselves, both in words and in the language of touch. And it was precisely the latter that he needed. He had even stepped out on her a few times in order to get some satisfaction in this regard. To no avail, as it turns out.

He did not just want sudden, explosive, nearly "perverse, excessive, and violent" encounters, but rather frequent little mutual signs of erotic love throughout the day. And she was afraid of "clinginess."

"I do believe I am jealous of the cat," he said suddenly during the third session, "because he gets stroked more than I do."

Those words were enough. For a moment it looked as though she would get very angry, then tears came to her eyes, and then she laughed right through them.

"O, my poor little tomcat," she said blushing, "if you had only told me earlier. How deprived you've been."

"Not at all! I have never been deprived. You . . ."

Quick, get home to invent and put into practice a new code.

Other Circles

Of course, there is also a touch code in other we-circles. At the first encounter, we give the right hand to those who were until recently unknown to us. Skin on skin. Then we know each other somewhat.

There are also another whole series of coded confidences, which vary from subculture to subculture. Very interesting and educational. But we will not pursue it further. We must add here, however, that if someone experiences some sexual desire upon touching someone who is not his or her lover — regardless of whether it be coded — it is wise, for practical reasons, to put an immediate end to it.

The experience is the result of the previously mentioned "erotic fascination." In and of itself it is neither good nor bad, because it is a reflex. But giving in to it can lead to irreparable damage. (And whoever — lover or no lover — experiences such feelings with his own or someone else's children stands on the verge of incest or sexual abuse. The line is clearly demarcated; no one needs to cross it.)

Caring

Whoever is not careful and attentive in loving interaction does not really love.

Caring is always present when we are open to the needs of the other and try to meet them. May the beloved then lack nothing? She must have her desires, her ego must be established, and her heart must have joy.

That is why lovers try, as far as they are able, to be caring toward each other. That is not a duty but a privilege. If caring happens to entail a certain degree of repetitiveness, so what?

Financial and material care can be provided from a distance. But this is a seldom mentioned aspect except when it is lacking. Caring almost always concerns the little things that are close at hand.

"He just does not notice," my niece says, the one I have not seen in years.

Yes, that indeed seems to be the case, from what she has told me. He does not notice that she is sometimes tired. He does not sit her down on the couch with a cup of coffee and the newspaper so that he can pick up the mess and do the dishes himself. He hardly remembers her birthday. He never just buys her silly little gifts. "No, he just does not notice."

Even less does he notice that it is raining, and that she has gone out without a jacket and an umbrella. And so forth. The man is blind. Nothing seems to penetrate to him, and if it should per chance penetrate, it does not set him into action. (And even worse for my family, he never polishes her shoes, not when solicited and especially not when unsolicited.)

If he does not notice anything — not the dog, not the plants, not the things in and around the house — *how can she know that he has a heart?* Because he makes love so wonderfully and babbles so passionately about the environment?

Accepting Care

Caring about each other, in the big and in the little, ordinary things, as well as providing care for others and for something other than ourselves: this is a kind of sign language, just like touch. Here too is an irreplaceable means of sharing how we must approach each other's heart.

That is why lovers must *accept care* from each other. With that I mean that the one must enjoy it when the other wants to give care and attention. In the double center, trust is complete; thus also in this regard.

"But I can do it myself a lot faster and better. Besides, I do not want him to spoil me." That is a completely different tune than the one my niece sang. But here too there is something important at work. This is the way her husband seeks, in his own way, to communicate something important to her. He tries to do nice things for her.

She should give him a kiss and look happy when he comes home from work earlier than expected in order to do yesterday's dishes and to pick up the house before she arrives home. But he receives no kiss and she looks at him suspiciously. She calls it spoiling. But what is wrong with (mutual) spoiling?

Why is she being so difficult? Because she is one of those people who always has to find something to complain about? Because she had a mother who spoiled her? Yes, that appears to have been the case again.

We apparently should add a variant to the first sentence of this section: *whoever does not accept care does not know what true love is.*

Other Circles

In other, wider circles, the amount of trust is less and the character is different. And so is the care.

What was earlier said about the special place of children is equally true here. At first they are completely part of the double center and remove themselves, gradually, to the A-circle. If they are raised in a caring environment, they will — insofar as it is possible — take on the care of themselves, of the other, and of other things.

The traditional division of labor of Adam, who must work, and Eve, who must do the wash, is out of date and unusable. Yet it will be a couple of generations before we are beyond it, because most people have the irretractable tendency to raise their children as they themselves were raised.

Sometimes a(n unspoken) request for care comes from one of the wider circles, from someone who is not able (anymore) to care for himself. If it is somehow possible, the request is usually honored, but in a way that is proper to the we-circle from which it derived.

If one does not pay attention to the boundaries of the circles, damage later occurs. *Whoever helps care for another may not pull him into a we-circle in which there is, in the long run, no place for him.* If that happens, something of the hard truth from the old Armenian saying will be brought to bear: "Think hard before you save someone's life. He will forever hold you responsible for all the misery that he suffers and you must protect and maintain him for the rest of his life, or else he will poison you."

But the rabbis were also right — as they always were. "Whoever saves a man's life saves with him all of mankind."

The Meal

The basic forms of loving interaction overlap one another. The meal is a good example: it is care, and at the same time a unique, irreplaceable way to give people a sense that they belong together. The bond with the gods is also experienced in this way in the primitive offering meals of nearly all religions.

In mutual dependence, we vulnerably come together, not only to stave our hunger and quench our thirst. (With great vegetative pressure of hunger or thirst, it is even sometimes impossible to have a meal.) It is a question of more. Lovers want to enjoy one another's company. They try to please each other, to let the other be himself or herself, to act from the heart, and perhaps in so doing they become aware of something of the wonder.

Those who truly hold a meal are there for each other and make that clear. They break bread and drink wine — for each other. *For each other.* That is the essence. The table is the prerequisite for the bed. *Ein Liebespaar is wie es iszt.*

The Dishes

The oft-heard spats over the dishes are terribly old-fashioned and beneath any standard. A meal is only complete if it is — in a simple and broad way — a love meal. It begins in the store and ends with the cleaning up and the dishes. Sometimes these are done alone, for the other, and sometimes they are done together, depending on how it turns out. Those who have not already made it part of their code would do well to do so quickly.

Those who have never made the effort to provide, as far as is possible, a complete meal do not know what true love is. (Quit your complaining! If you can read, you can cook too.)

Refrigerator and Microwave Relationships

Overloaded and unsynchronized calendars, along with the totalitarian claims of the market and institutions, have made the complete meal almost impossible. That has a centrifugal effect on the double center.

People who are experiencing problems with each other often also appear, by virtue of their circumstances, to have let things get to the point where they have already separated themselves "from the table." Sometimes they even have the gall to ask me why it is that things no longer are going so well in bed. They have lapsed into a *refrigerator and microwave relationship*. There is hardly any élan vital invested in the mealtimes anymore as an indispensable basic form of loving interaction. Those who hunger and thirst grab fast food and *fend for themelves*, without taking any notice of time or place.

Those who choose such a lifestyle may do so, but may not blame the other if the flame of love dies out. (Moreover, he loses the right to pontificate about love!)

Three complete meals per day appears to be out of the question in this day and age, but five times a week is a minimum — not including "let's just order Chinese."

Furthermore, it is advisable to disconnect the doorbell and the telephone, since appointment makers and bill collectors prefer to show up at mealtime.

"But professor," said a slight woman with a short gray haircut and fierce eyes, "you are always talking about the material aspect. Is love not spiritual?"

I do not like the dualism that lurks behind her words, but this time I wanted to follow her. "Madam," I said, "I am deeply convinced that there is nothing more spiritual than a meal."

Play

Playing together — but here in the broadest possible sense — is even less dispensable as fuel for the fire of love.

It is walking through a different — sometimes more, sometimes less fixed — code. People can interact here in a very unique, open way with each other, seeking and finding.

In play, lovers are never opponents. Sometimes it appears that way, but that is only role playing. They are definitely playing together. If that is not the case, play becomes contest, which is foreign to the essence of love.

Giving a performance can be even less the purpose of play; at best it can be a means of enhancing the fun.

The word *fun* is for me the primary characteristic of the world of play. It can be a question of nothing other than the pleasure of play.

The everyday world is left behind for a time and it is from that point on simply fun. Whether we are talking of playing cards, tennis, guessing games, singing songs, telling stories, performing plays (like crazy Bert and his bunch of flowers standing suddenly at the front door), or of various hobby-like activities, or high-level artistic endeavors — it matters not. As long as we, regularly or irregularly, simply play together. (That added "simply" is an essential condition. Those who do not fulfill this requirement confuse means and ends and degrade play into contest or performance. I know of surprisingly many bridge couples for whom that has become the case. Then play is no longer fun, and it can have a centrifugal effect.)

Work

Working together is also among the basic forms. By that is meant exerting oneself in order to produce something or perform something. Although working and playing can overlap, in this case they stand over against each other; in essence, playing is "having fun" and working is "achieving something."

Every love covenant should also include something of a work community, but in the modern families not too much comes of it. It is nice enough if from time to time the housekeeping or maintenance chores are taken on together. Just so long as it happens, and so long as the "together" is not limited to "I do it and you help me."

Making Love

"I am not coming next time," she said to the other members of the choir, "because my friend and I will be making love."

There was a moment of confusion, because everyone was thinking the same thing: *You make love in bed.* You do not plan it a week in advance and you certainly do not tell the choir about it.

Yet this common use of the phrase is dangerous and misleading. If she had said, "My friend and I are going to our new house to lay the carpet," everyone would have been satisfied.

Most people will have difficulty saying that love-making can also consist of laying carpet together, even though the experience is not strange to them.

Dreaming Together

The worlds of play and work are more or less encoded. Those who break the rules of play ruin the game. Those who ignore the rules of work do not render a good performance.

The world of imagination, where dreams are woven, knows no codes. It is entirely creative in nature. It must definitely not be confused with the proximate world of illusion, where circumstances, the empirically perceptible facts, are not recognized.

It is the world where the Great Longing is perceived *beyond the facts* through the imagination. That is why, as we said earlier, the dreams that are dreamt here are not the dreams of sleep, but rather are visionary dreams, which plead to be rendered reality.

Sometimes that plea is granted, and the dream becomes part of our everyday life. Sometimes only a part of the dream can be realized. Sometimes none of it is made reality due to the recalcitrance of the circumstances. But these dreams, which recognize facts but do not accept them and are able to see beyond them, these dreams can remain alive in faith, hope, and love.

That is why it is essential that lovers share their dreams with each other and also dream dreams and see visions together. Whether we are talking of nature or culture, of the divine, beauty, truth, peace, wholeness, or holiness, or all of the above, there must be a communal aspect to our dreams.

If that is not the case, we run the risk of ending up in the realm of Narcissus w.d., the land of the consumer.

Traveling

It is a primitive, basic form of loving: stepping out together, crossing the horizon, finding adventure, experiencing new things, and then returning home again enriched, as "new people."

But traveling does not only mean moving about in space. It especially means in this connection crossing horizons and experiencing new things together.

That can occur in many areas of life — as long as we hold each other by the hand and do not lose sight of our destination: coming back home enriched. (There are quite a few obscure stories about people who lose each other in a foreign land or who cannot find their way back home. They do not enter into the picture here.)

Sometimes lovers travel *separately* and share their experiences together upon return. One to the mountains, the other to the sea. So long as they also go together from time to time, that can certainly have a centripetal effect.

Sometimes the journey must be left *outside* of the realm of love. One or the other must take a course for work or study that cannot be shared with the lover. Earlier, in the section on one's own life, we noted that such activities must be as limited as possible. They quickly become solitary journeys to a world of meaning and experience to which the lover has no access. If it is unavoidable, it must be complemented with a journey together, in which *more* is experienced *more deeply* than on the solo flight.

The Look

In love, no couple can survive without looking at each other and reading the wonderful truth in each other's eyes.

The look of the lover is utterly symptomatic, and therefore so encouraging — fuel for the fire.

Nevertheless, I prefer that the glance also become part of the code. Take time to allow the visage of the lover to penetrate once again to the innermost parts. In this way the dream image remains alive and connected with everyday reality. To look through the flaws to the other's true nature is an act of creativity. People who do it regularly never grow tired of looking at each other.

The Word: Poetic and Deep

Lovers must also exchange words in order to make each other understand how great their love is.

These are not informative, technical, argumentative, or negotiating words, but rather — and especially — *poetic* words, because that which lovers actually want to say to each other can only be contained in stuttering allusions.

Not everyone is a poet, not to mention a good poet, yet it is still necessary to attempt on a regular basis to put into words what one is experiencing in the heart. Every time that the lover says something loving, the reality is creatively changed. Then the sun shines. In this day and age we are not so prone to believe in blessings and curses, but that does not mean that they do not work. Everyone knows how an unexpected good word can determine our existence.

(Thomas? Oh, yes, Thomas. For him, though, love is not a fire but a microwave.)

Deep words must also be spoken from time to time, words about life and death.

Lovers will one day lose each other to death; that is a part of life. It is horrible, but inevitable.

They can also lose each other to nonlife. That is the true death, which destroys love. This death can and must be avoided. In order to do so, deep words are a requisite.

A Weary Language

Previous generations had things much easier in this regard. In those days there existed a general language of belief and mystery that pointed beyond time and space. By means of this language, people were able to speak to each other in a very intimate way about the unspeakable.

This language, full of poetic and deep words, has been worn out by the misuse of hypocrites and fanatics. "The language of Canaan," it was later mockingly called.

Totally useless now, especially for those who have turned away from customary religious traditions. But who will give them new, deep words in order to understand each other regarding life and death?

Is that necessary? I believe it is. I know too many young couples, for example, who are confronted with the birth of a severely handicapped or even a dead child. Of course, there are no words for such things, but neither can one fail to speak about them. And so many of them lose each other in the very moment when they need each other most.

There are also too many older couples who have never held such deep discussions. When things suddenly come right down to it — and sooner or later they always do — they suddenly discover for the first time in their lives that they do not know what to say to each other.

Poems, which have always been read with sympathy and emotion, can perhaps fill the void that has appeared as a result of the disappearance of the language of Canaan. The text of pop songs can have the same effect (Lenny Kravitz!).

But here again it is a necessary precondition that those who make use of them — in better days — have experienced something of which the poems or the pop songs speak.

Time-Knot Rituals

Circumstances regularly appear in life that create a knot in *time*. (Not clock time, but experience time.) A kind of condensation and interweaving of the past, the present, and the future.

That is the case, for example, for those who pass from one stage of life to another, whether it be in the wake of a crucial decision or not. When one begins (a new) school, the first job, leaving the parental home, getting married or moving in with someone, the birth of a child, ego-loss, etc.

After such a change, things will never be as they were before. Something is definitively over, but the new is not yet present. The danger is great — even after a conscious crucial decision — that a person remains entangled in the knot of past, present, and future.

One of the causes of this — one that has already been mentioned — is the *imperfect-past tense*. Those who suffer this malady are unable to go any further. But it is also possible that people remain entangled because they do not quite know how to take the next step, and therefore keep postponing it.

In order to be able to escape such a time knot (passage, transition, threshold),[3] every traditional (sub)culture has had at its disposal, since antiquity, certain *rituals;* that is, the coded, symbolic actions of a (large or small) community. *Their goal is to make those who must move on to a new stage into new persons, and to make the community a new community that can move on with them.* In that way they have, once again through covenant, a perspective on the future. (Celebration is here understood as an expanded ritual, in which use is made of several dialogical basic forms.)

With the senses, ego, and heart, it is possible to *experience* how (first of all) the previous stage of life has been completed, and how (secondly) the dangerous middle ground has been safely traversed, and how (thirdly) a new beginning has been made possible for everyone by ushering in and initiating the new stage of life. (These three steps are minimally necessary.)

It is continually clearer that no one can ignore the time knots in life with impunity. The power of a ritual must certainly not be underestimated. The benefit of ritual mourning, for example, is slowly being recognized by everyone. Yet much less value has been attached to the ritual establishment of a love covenant. Very unwise.

There is a good chance that those who do not care to make the investment will still pay later, with interest — whether to a therapist or to a lawyer. Both very ritual figures.

3. See van der Hart and Nieuwkoop in the bibliography.

The Benefit of Marriage

It is not a question, for me, whether people should formally sanction their marriage. That is something that we, in this individualized society, happily may decide for ourselves.

For me it is the fact that the beginning of a love covenant must be, for practical reasons, ritually marked, celebrated. Those who do not feel — for whatever reason — comfortable with the existing customs must invent and encode their own, after studying Indian or Tibetan wedding rituals for example, if need be.

The three above-mentioned *steps* must be taken carefully into account, as was noted above. Moreover, the persons from the A- and B-circles must stand as witnesses of the event, *because it is with them that one must move on in the new relationship*.

Whatever is done ought to have a symbolic character. That means, above all, that *as many senses and as many basic forms must be put to use* as possible. (Eros must have his way. Nothing enters the heart that has not first been in the senses.) Touching, eating and drinking, play in various forms, including music, dance, and theater, traveling, and speeches. All these "allusions" must also refer to the *world of meaning* of the allusion. If that is not the case, it might as well not be done. (Narcissus must feel at home. Nothing enters the heart that has no meaning for the ego. That is why, at least in the Netherlands, it is better to comply with local custom and to be somewhat careful with Indian and Tibetan rituals.)

But the power of a ritual reaches beyond its meaning. Suddenly, but not just like that, the kairos appears, the golden moment. The wind begins to blow, the hearts of the lovers and the witnesses leap for joy. One becomes faintly aware of the ineffable mystery, the wonder of love, the clear of life. Everyone is suddenly transcendently beautiful. The members of the orchestra are themselves transported by the music they make. Outside, the nightingales or the thrushes — depending on the time of day — sing beautifully. The flowers that the bride carries begin to shine and spread their aroma with renewed strength, and even the gifts of tin and copper begin to shine like silver and gold.

That is the practical benefit of the wedding. Everyone and everything becomes an accomplice, even the god who is invoked as witness. (Therefore it is of utmost importance to choose the very best for such an occasion.)

All those who are present as witnesses at such a celebration renew their own covenant by their very participation. And those who have none become vaguely aware of the Light of the Star of Hope.

In this way love covenants are made and renewed. Only in this way.

Spiritual Rituals

In addition to knots, the timeline displays a number of large and small spirals: the years with their seasons, the months with their phases of the moon, the weeks with their days, mealtimes, sunrises, and sunsets.

For me these are not signs of the eternal return of things. I do not see time as cyclical, not as a wheel, a pretzel, or a snake that bites its tail, but as a spiral that winds toward the end of time.

That is why people encounter many transitions that present themselves in spiral fashion. They appear as the *rhythm* of (experiential) time. It is a primitive wisdom that one cannot just casually pass through these spiral transitions. That must occur with full self-consciousness; otherwise one loses a grip on (experiential) time, in spite of a perfectly maintained schedule. Then one easily loses an essential dimension of reality consciousness.

Those who do not take (experiential) time are mercilessly taken by (clock) time. "I feel so stressed out!" people say today. That cannot bode well; not in life and certainly not in love. That is why all cultures have ritually encoded these transitions.

Many modern people get nothing out of the symbolism of the — often religious — traditional rituals. It could also be the case that people now have a life rhythm that no longer resonates with the life rhythms of the agrarian society in which many of these rituals arose. (The bell no longer rings in the distance. "Thanksgiving day for the crops" has no significance for apartment dwellers with no garden of their own.)

If that is the case, something else must replace them: *spiritual rituals*. These are celebrations and other rituals that mark and make possible the rhythmically appearing spiral transitions of (experiential) time. Superficial customs, without any possible reference to meaning and mystery, are utterly insufficient.

"I Want Mine with a Kiss"

To give just one example: the transition of day and night is a confused jumble in most modern families — that is easy to understand, but for practical reasons, not good ones.

It is and remains a dramatic transition. Biologically, several different systems must be engaged in a short period of time, and that is easier for some than for others. Moreover, harmful tensions must be replaced with the creative tensions that are necessary for achievement.

This simply *may* not occur without spiritual rituals. No lover may leave the house or stay home alone without something warm in the stomach, without a kiss, without a good word, without a wave.

And if a lunch must be packed, no one must prepare it for himself or herself. Because bread spread with love is more than food.

"How do you like your eggs in the morning?" someone asks in a song to a(n apparently very young) lover. That is a good start, but the answer shows even more wisdom and insight into the morning ritual: "I want mine with a kiss."

She likes eggs, but she would also accept bread with jam. "As long as I get my kiss." My kiss — exactly.

Of course things could also be very different, depending on the (sub)culture and the world of meaning and experience. Just so long as it occurs. I know of couples who every morning ritually take a shower together. No one can allow with impunity the lover to simply slip away in the morning without having had love.

You do not agree? Still, spiral rituals are there precisely in order to keep Thorndike's flywheel of love spinning, whether you agree or not.

The At-work/At-home Transition

The transition from work to home appears to be just as difficult for many couples. Yet it takes place each day, with extra emphasis on the weekends and during vacations.

211

If the transition is not successfully made, one remains *imprisoned in a form of self-consciousness that is not appropriate to the situation.* Love cannot then come into her own right. Taking work home from the office in order to leisurely finish it at home is something totally different. That can sometimes be quite aggravating for the lover, but that is not the point here. Here we are dealing with the fact that one must attempt to set aside the competitive, achievement-oriented work attitude and especially the language associated with it.

The Three Steps

Usually he arrives first. He sets out two glasses and walks around to pick up a bit until he hears her.

She is accustomed, after giving him a somewhat absent kiss, to giving him her purse and coat and plopping down in a chair. Then she says, "How was your day?"

He brings her things into the front hall, turns on the CD player, goes to the refrigerator to take out the sherry bottle, and tells her in few words something of his day. Then he sits down facing her.

She pours and tells him about her own day. They both take their glasses, but wait to drink until everything has been said.

If that takes a long time, they set their glasses down again, but if one of them becomes too long-winded, the other will say: "Hurry up, darling, I need a drink."

"All right," the other then says, "Just a minute. I . . ." and then follows a bit more. At this point step one is over. They take a drink and say: "Ah," or "wonderful," or "here we are again," and laugh trustingly with each other.

When the glasses are empty, she usually turns the CD player off and brings the glasses to the sink. He puts the bottle back in the refrigerator (after quickly having snuck a clandestine sip) and goes to wash his hands. She usually puts something else on and then step two is over.

One of the two now says something like: "Come, get cozy here by me, I need a hug. I have not seen you all day. Do you still love me?"

Yes, that is still the case.

That was step three, and then they go about their own activities.

This ritual turns them into different people, who are again completely there for each other. They have not really reflected on it; it has grown up out of their seeking each other and has become encoded. The CD player that sits ready is part of it, just as is the trusting laugh, which points to many precious memories and more. But only after the hug are they really together again. If the ritual must be skipped for whatever reason, they miss it, and have trouble hitting their stride.

It can also follow a completely different pattern, and some couples can live without it, but not this one. Even if they arrive home tired and in a bad mood, they know that they will again be coming home to a different self-consciousness, one appropriate to love.

Other Spiral Transitions

Moving from one basic form to another, ending the day, beginning and ending the week, beginning and ending vacations, changes of seasons and years, birthdays, joyful and sad memorials — they are all just so many changes in our experiential time, changes that lovers are not always certain how to handle.

Spontaneously improvise? Sometimes there is enough élan vital and then it certainly must be attempted. In that way people gain important experiences, which can eventually be encoded into rituals.

But it will not always work. *Nor must it.* Rousseau is only partly right, and the oft-praised free expression has brought many to misery. We all find ourselves empty from time to time, and in the words of Pestalozzi, "not even the hawk and the eagle can steal eggs from the nest if the nest has no eggs." Couples who cannot or will not make use of traditional rituals would do well to create rituals themselves for their own personal use. That is not easy, but it is a price that must be paid for the greater good of the individualization and personalization of existence.

Shulamite Day

Under the influence of the many centrifugal forces — the cracks in the mosaic of existence and all the other obscure things — all love covenants wear out. That is why they must regularly be *renewed.* That is an essential condition for love.

One must not wait until one of the two — or both — have turned away, because then there is little more that can be done. The fire must be stirred and new fuel must be provided while it is still burning.

Spontaneously or ritually (I recommend the latter), everything must again be brought into the light of full self-consciousness: *desire, fascination, and response (Eros); longing, being struck by, and choosing (Narcissus); yearning, illumination, being set in the flame and the fire, and deciding definitively (Shulamite).*

Then the blessings, the promises, and the intentions can be repeated and confirmed with a peaceful heart. In so doing, all that has gone wrong in the past is undone. A sort of Day of Atonement, literally and figuratively.

Some kind of celebrative meal should be part of it, of course, as should looking at pictures and videotapes, and perhaps a small pilgrimage to the place where it all began. It also seems good to me to read the Song of Songs together on the couch in the evening by candlelight and incense. One can, of course, think of more and other wonderful things, just as long as it happens. Everyone can pick an appropriate date for such a covenant renewal. Those who have been formally married will use their anniversary. Those who have made their covenant in a different fashion will take the day that was experienced as the crucial point or the time knot.

I have an even better idea. We have a Mother's Day and a Father's Day and a Remembrance Day and a Valentine's Day. Why don't we call the second Sunday of February *Shulamite Day,* the day on which all lovers ritually renew their covenants? That way, after so many centuries, she will receive the honor she deserves, and with her every woman who — consciously or unconsciously — has been inspired by her. In the middle of February it still gets dark relatively early in the evening, with an eye on the candlelight. And at that time of year, when the air is clear, a beautiful star-filled sky is visible, with an eye on the Star of Hope. To that can be added that it is still cold enough to light a fire in the fireplace,

214

with an eye on the Fire of Love. The last is true, to be sure, only for those who are fortunate enough to possess a fireplace, but maybe we can think of something comparable to the community bonfire. (And finally, it just happens to be the weekend on which Els and I made our crucial decision.)

11. Afterword

The Young Man in the White Jacket Again

I cannot sleep, so finally I go downstairs to put on some tea and to smoke my pipe and to attempt to find a different self-consciousness with the help of a comforting book.

It is a beautiful and peaceful summer night. In an hour or so the birds will begin to sing to welcome the first light of the sun. They do that every morning; those who have never heard it have really missed something.

I sit thinking that the animals naturally have no self-consciousness and therefore no hope in the future. They must give up the hope every night that it will ever be light again. When the slightest glimmer of light appears on the eastern horizon, they immediately burst out in ecstatic joy, as if they had risen from the dead. From the dead!

Then I see him suddenly: the young man in the white jacket, with whom I began this book. I had only seen the words on his back during a television report on an AIDS demonstration. *Can we accept a society where we are deathly afraid to love?*

Actually, I thought he was already out of my mind. I thought it was just all that outdated, faddish drivel of those superficial sex consumers who are even too lazy to take reasonable measures for their own protection. And when things go wrong, then suddenly the society has failed. How? Is the product-testing service corrupt?

Such people should not be taken seriously.

Or should they?

Then I came to the conclusion that it was a question of homonyms

216

— two different meanings for the same word; in this case, "love." He means sex, and I mean agape. I need pay no heed to what he has to say, because sex is not my subject.

Yet I am apparently not yet rid of him, because he is sitting there in front of me again. Now no longer with his back to me — with those silly words written on the back of his jacket — but for the first time we see each other face-to-face.

We seem to know each other well; he is my father, my brother, my son.

"Wait a minute," I protest, before he can say anything. "I never condemned you. As a matter of fact, this book was written to reach you. Read it. Then you will see what I mean. I must admit, it is somewhat biased — unintentionally, unintentionally. It makes a distinction between those who long for true love and those who despise it, or are unable to experience it." (I am, of course, part of the good group, but that is just a coincidence.) "It is really a question of the restoration of love for me, not the surreptitious justification of a certain lifestyle."

He just looks at me and answers nothing. And so I carry on a lengthy monologue that sounds less and less convincing to me.

Suddenly he lifts his hand and I can stop. We listen.

Apparently the birds outside have seen the glimmer of light on the eastern horizon, for they burst out in a deafening warble, trill, chirp, tweet, and whistle. As though their lives depended on it.

And it does.

We look at each other with understanding. Finally.

Then we laugh, relieved. We go outside together, put an arm around each other's shoulder, and whistle along.

But not nearly so impressively as the birds.

Bibliography

A list of literary references is inevitably long, boring, and furthermore incomplete.

Many of the thoughts in this book are not my own. They just blew in my direction. But who was it that released them in the first place, so that the wind could blow them my way? I often do not know. I am often aware that I have heard them before, but where and when eludes me.

It is not my intention, however, consciously to fail to give anyone credit.

Barthes, R. *Fragments d'un discours amoureux.* Paris, 1976. Published in English as *A Lover's Discourse: Fragments.* Translated by Richard Howard. New York: Hill and Wang, 1978.

——. *Roland Barthes by Roland Barthes.* Translated by Richard Howard. New York: Hill and Wang, 1977.

Bataille, G. *Der heilige Eros* [Holy Eros]. Frankfurt/Berlin/Vienna, 1974.

Berger, W. J., et al. *Het veranderende beeld van huwelijk, relaties en scheiding: Maatschappelijke en godsdienstige aspecten* [The changing image of marriage, relationships and divorce]. Delft, 1983.

Bergson, H. L. *The Two Sources of Morality and Religion.* Translated by R. A. Audra and C. Brereton, with the assistance of W. Horsfall Carter. New York: H. Holt and Co., 1936.

Boswijk-Hummel, R. *De anatomie van liefde* [The anatomy of love]. Haarlem, 1990.

Bouritius, G. et al. *Religieuze ervaring: Een veelvormig perspectief op de zin van het bestaan* [Religious experience: A polymorphic perspective on the meaning of existence]. Tilburg, 1988.

Buytendijk, F. J. J. *De onbevangenheid* [Openness]. Bilthoven, 1973.

218

Cats, Jacob. *Sinne en minnebeelden* [The senses and the image of the lover] and *Spiegel van den ouden en nieuwen tijdt* [Mirror of the old and new era]. Amsterdam, 1665; reprint, Den Haag, 1977.

Coenen, H. *Door kou bevangen: Zelfdoding en nabestaanden* [Overcome by the cold: Suicide and the survivors]. Baarn, 1989.

de Boer, A. P. *Partnerdoding: Een empirisch forensisch-psychiatrisch onderzoek* [Partnercide: An empirical forensic-psychiatric investigation]. Dissertation, Nijmegen, 1990.

de Groot, Maria. *Messiaanse ikonen* [Messianic icons]. Kampen, 1987.

de Jong, A. *Een onbesproken kinderwereld: Opgroeien in een armoedetraditie* [An untold world of children: Growing up in the poverty tradition]. Utrecht, 1990.

Dekker, A. and J. H. Dijkman. *Samen-leven: Theologisch-etische verkenning van alternatieve tweerelaties als bijdrage tot een pastorale benadering* [Living together: A theological-ethical exploration of alternative partner relationships as a contribution to a pastoral approach]. Kampen, 1982.

de Lorris, Guillaume. See A. van Altena.

Dresen, G. *Onschuldfantasieën: Offerzin en heilsverlangen in feminisme en mystiek* [Fantasies of innocence: A sense of sacrifice and the longing for salvation in feminism and mysticism]. Nijmegen, 1990.

Droste, F. G. *Bij wijze van spreken: Over gedrag, taal en communicatie* [So to speak: On behavior, language and communication]. Baarn, 1977.

Eco, U. *A Theory of Semiotics*. Bloomington: Indiana University Press, 1976.

Finkielkraut, A. *La sagesse d'amour* [The wisdom of love]. Paris, 1984.

Foucault, M. *Die sorge um ich: Sexualität und Wahrheit* [Concern for myself: Sexuality and truth]. Frankfurt, 1981.

Freud, S. *Gesammelte Werke* [Collected works], especially volume 8, *Beitrage zur psychologie des liebeslebens* [A contribution to the psychology of the love life]. See also volume 13, *Verliebtheit und hypnose* [Love and hypnosis]. Frankfurt am Main: S. Fischer, 1952-90.

Fromm, E. *The Art of Loving*. Mexico City, 1975.

Heidegger, M. *The Question of Being*. Translated by William Kluback and Jean T. Wilde. New York: Twayne Publishers, 1958.

Hekma, G. et al. *Het verlies van de onschuld: Sexualiteit in Nederland* [Loss of innocence: Sexuality in the Netherlands]. Groningen, 1990.

Huici, F. *Klimt*. Milan, 1989.

Kortram, L. *De culture van het oordelen* [The culture of judgment]. Dissertation, Nijmegen, 1990.

Kravitz, L. *Let Love Rule.* Compact disc CDVUS10, Virgin Records America, Inc., 1989.

Kristeva, J. *Histoires D'Amour.* Grenoble: Editions Denoel, 1983. Published in English translation as *Tales of Love.* Translated by Leon S. Roudiez. New York: Columbia University Press, 1987.

Kuenkel, F. *Einführung in die Charakterkunde auf individualpsychologischer grundlage* [Introduction to the science of character from an individual-psychological perspective]. Leipzig, 1928.

Levinas, E. *Difficult Freedom: Essays on Judaism.* Translated by Sean Hand. Baltimore: Johns Hopkins University Press, 1990.

———. *Ethics and Infinity.* Translated by Richard A. Cohen. Pittsburgh: Duquesne University Press, 1985.

———. *Existence and Existents.* The Hague, 1978.

———. *Otherwise Than Being: or, Beyond Essence.* Translated by Alphonso Lingis. Norwell, Mass.: Kluwer, 1981

Maeckelberghe, E. *Desperately Seeking Mary.* Dissertation, Kampen, 1991.

Marcuse, H. *Eros en Cultuur.* Utrecht, 1970.

Meihuizen, J. *De kunst der vrijage* [Ovid's *Ars Amatoria*]. Den Haag, 1941.

Meulenbelt, A. *De schaamte voorbij: Een persoonlijke geschiedenis* [Beyond shame: A personal history]. Amsterdam, 1977.

———. *Casablanca of de onmogelijkheden van de heterosexuele liefde* [Casablanca, or the impossibilities of heterosexual love]. Amsterdam, 1990.

Nieuwkoop, R. *De drempel over: Het gebruik van (overgangs) rituelen in het pastoraat* [Over the threshold: The use of (transition) rituals in the pastorate]. Den Haag, 1986.

Nygren, A. *Agape and Eros.* Translated by Philip S. Watson. Chicago, 1982.

Ovid, *Metamorphoses.* Translated by Rolfe Humphries. Bloomington: Indiana University Press, 1955.

Pascal, Blaise. *Pascal's Pensées.* With an English translation, brief notes and introduction by H. F. Stewart. New York: The Modern Library, 1947.

Ricoeur, P. *Oneself as Another.* Translated by Kathleen Blamey. Chicago: University of Chicago Press, 1992.

Robin, L. *La théorie platonicienne de l'amour* [The platonic theory of love]. Paris, 1934.

Sartre, Jean-Paul. *Being and Nothingness: An Essay in Phenomenological Ontology.* Translated by Hazel E. Barnes. New York: Citadel Press, 1956.

———. *In Camera.* In *Two Plays.* Translated by Stuart Gilbert. London: H. Hamilton, 1946.

Schmitt, J. C. *La Raison des gestes dans l'occident médiéval* [The reason for gestures in the medieval West]. Paris, 1990.

Schreurs, K. *Vrouwen in lesbische relaties* [Women in lesbian relationships]. Dissertation, Utrecht, 1990.

Sebeok, T. A. *Contributions to the Doctrine of Signs.* Bloomington: Indiana University Press; Lisse, The Netherlands: P. De Ridder Press, 1976.

ter Horst, W. *Over troosten en verdriet* [On comfort and grief]. Kampen, 1991

———. *Het herstel van het gewone leven* [The restoration of the common life]. Groningen, 1988.

———. *Christelijke gelofsopvoeding* [Nurturing Christian faith]. Kampen, 1991.

———. *Algemene orthopedagogiek* [General orthopedagogy]. Kampen, 1980.

Thorndike, E. L. *Human Nature and the Social Order.* Cambridge, Mass.: MIT Press, 1969.

Toonder, M. "De feunix" [The phoenix]. In *Een heer moet alles alleen doen* [A gentleman must do everything alone]. Amsterdam, 1973.

Trachtenberg, P. *Het Casanova-complex: De dwangmatige verleider* [The Casanova complex: The compulsive seducer]. Amsterdam, 1990.

Trible, P. "Depatriarchalizing in Biblical Interpretation." *Journal of the American Academy of Religion* 41, no. 1 (1973).

———. *God and the Rhetoric of Sexuality.* Philadelphia: Fortress Press, 1978.

van Altena, E. *De Roman van de Roos, van Guillaume de Lorris en Jean de Meung* [The romance of the rose of Guillaume de Lorris and Jean de Meung]. Baarn, 1991. (A wonderful Dutch translation.)

van den Berg, A. A. *Als mensen door God worden aangeraakt* [When people are touched by God]. Dissertation, Brussels, 1988.

van der Hart, O. *Overgang en bestendiging* [Transition and permanence]. Arnhem, 1985.

van Kampen, K. D. *Tot liefde bevrijd: Liefde leren vanuit het hooglied* [Freed to love: Teachings on love from the Song of Songs]. Den Haag, 1980.

Wach, J. *Vergleichende Religionsforschung* [The comparative study of religion]. Stuttgart, 1962.

Widdershoven, G. A. M. and T. Boer (ed.). *Hermeneutiek in discussie* [Hermeneutic in discussion]. Amsterdam, 1990.

Winkler, J. *The Constraints of Desire: The Anthropology of Sex and Gender in Ancient Greece.* New York: Routledge, 1990.